The Control Book

By Peter Masters

Copyright © 2006, Peter Masters

All rights reserved. No part of this book may be reproduced or transmitted in any form or by any means, electronic or mechanical, including photocopying, recording, or by any informational storage or retrieval system, except with permission in writing from the author.

Also by Peter Masters:
Look Into My Eyes
This Curious Human Phenomenon

Cover art by Peter Masters

http://www.peter-masters.com/

Published by Custom Books Publishing, 2009

ISBN 978-1-4421-7386-6

The Control Book

Contents

1 Introduction   **1**
    1.1   What do you mean by dominance & submission?   7
    1.2   Conscious, subconscious and unconscious   11
    1.3   Predispositions   23
    1.4   Evolution   37

2 Control   **47**
    2.1   The process   49
    2.2   Consolidating control   59
    2.3   Losing control   65
    2.4   Reward and encouragement   73
    2.5   Giving back control   77
    2.6   Focus of control   83
    2.7   Safewords   89
    2.8   Control-taking and privacy   95

3 Communication   **99**
    3.1   Division of labour   101
    3.2   Submissive logic   105
    3.3   Person-to-person   111
    3.4   Three   117

4 Management   **123**
    4.1   Two different types of control   125
    4.2   Planning and management   129

	4.3	Ritual	143
	4.4	Structure	149
	4.5	Ownership	157
	4.6	Delegation	161

5 Discussion topics   167

5.1	Closure	169
5.2	Magic	171
5.3	Satiation	173
5.4	Humour	175
5.5	Rhythm	177
5.6	Feeling controlled	179
5.7	Consequences of orders	181
5.8	Difference between a slave and a submissive . . .	183
5.9	Cookbook dominance	185
5.10	Less than open	187
5.11	What place love?	189
5.12	Hard and soft limits	191

Chapter 1

Introduction

Mastery isn't just telling someone what to do. It's also creating the environment in which your submissive will do what you want even without being told. It is creating an environment in which they have only the one choice, and that is of doing what you want.

I want to come right out and say that this isn't a definitive textbook. I didn't write it to be one.

I'm a sadist at heart, and I have learned that one of the cruelest things you can do to someone is to teach them something, and thereby cause them to question their ignorance and long-held beliefs. As you're actually looking at this voluntarily, then it's likely that you're not the sort who's going to be particularly traumatised by being made to think. That's a shame, but on the off chance that you're looking at this book by mistake, I will attempt, in the following pages and chapters, to stir up some new thoughts, and to cause you to reflect on many things that you've probably just taken for granted up until now. I hope, by the end of the book, that you'll have a new understanding and appreciation for what control actually is—particularly in the context of BDSM—and how to use it.

BDSM is an abbreviation for Bondage & Discipline, Dominance & Submission and Sadism & Masochism. These are areas of often-sexual activity involving pain, restraint, confinement, and authority. This is, of course, a very general definition, and doesn't convey either the extent of activities called "BDSM", or the range of emotions, passions and just broad psychological responses which BDSM can inspire.

One very important thing is that BDSM activities are rarely done solo. BDSM works best when there are two people, one of whom has the explicit role of being in control of what goes on. This fact lies at the heart of this book.

In all sincerity, I don't expect you to agree with everything I have to say in this book. Your experience and your preferences might cause you to look at what I say and decide that it's the biggest load of rubbish that modern waste-management techniques have ever had to deal with. No matter. If it succeeds in at least making you reflect on your own views—even if you just end up confirming them—then I'll be able to go to the great writers' home in the sky happy.

I believe that a very large part of the activities, which we include under the umbrella of BDSM, rely explicitly or implicitly on control being asserted over one person by another. These people are variously called *tops, bottoms, dominants, submissives, masters, mistresses, slaves,* and so on. However, what they're called isn't that important. What is important is how they use control. My goal in this book is to talk about control, explain what it is, demonstrate it, show how to take it, how to give it, how to manage it, and more. I want you, the reader, to be aware of the ebb and flow of control around you and through you.

Control is something that is present in many or most BDSM activities. It's explicit in many or most dominance & submission activities and lifestyles, and is usually obvious-to-a-blind-man in many bondage scenes, floggings, pain-play, piercings, and similar activities, where part of the thrill for one person is placing themselves in the hands (or control) of the other and just letting go.

For many people, control is like a tool or a catalyst. These people might be into the sexual thrills that they can get via their scenes, or the endorphin rush from heavy pain-play, or the subspace; and they use control as part of how they achieve this. Control, for these people, is not what they look for. They might not even realise the part which control plays in what they do.

Then there are people for whom control is THE BIG THING. Dominants and submissives, as well as some masters and slaves, are usually good examples of these people. Their main interest is in explicitly controlling or being controlled by their partner. Pain, bondage, and so on become tools used to impose, or demonstrate, or manipulate control. These are the people I'm interested in. I refer to them, or the relationships where the element of control is primary, as *control-sensitive*. Control here is not a want, but a need.

As I'm going to be spending a lot of time talking about control, I'd like to make it clear exactly what it is that I'm talking about. The Oxford English Dictionary (OED) defines *control* (the verb) as: *To exercise restraint or direction upon the free action of; to hold sway over, exercise power or authority over; to dominate, command.*

I am interested in all of this, mainly in the context of one person controlling another. I won't be talking about things like blackmail or threats as a way of achieving control, nor will I be talking about using physical force to control someone[1]. This still leaves a lot of ground for us to cover.

The book is divided into five chapters. The first chapter—this present one—is called **Introduction**. This is where I'll be

---

[1] Controlling someone by physical force—i.e. using overwhelming strength to force them to do what you want—is different to taking control of someone using physical force—i.e. using physical force to claim control. If this isn't clear, I will be looking at this latter case, but not the former, later in the book.

doing the groundwork: defining terms and providing background, which will hopefully make the rest of the book easier to digest. It is also where I explain what I think is a quaint relationship between evolution and dominance & submission.

The following chapter, **Transfer Of Control**, is fairly meaty. It's where I'll be talking about what's involved in taking control, giving up control, losing control, maintaining control, giving back control, delegating control, what can go wrong as control is being transferred, etc. It's the raw mechanics.

After that is a chapter on **Communication**. I know that every man and his dog has written something on communication, but there are some aspects unique to dominance & submission which are very important, but which are also rarely considered. I'll be looking at some of them here, including control of communication, plus communication and the impact on it of different headspaces or states of mind which can occur, such as *sub-space*.

Sub-space, in fewer words than necessary to do it justice, is a typically inwardly-focussed state of mind accompanied by emotional or spiritual feelings such as loss of identity, floating, feelings of belonging, being protected, and desire to please the dominant.

The last main chapter of the book is about **Management**. People involved in isolated scenes at play-parties don't face the same issues which far-reaching and long-term dominant & submissive relationships have to deal with. In this chapter I look at things like maintaining the feeling of control in the absence of the dominant, and long-term service issues.

I end the book with a small(?) chapter of **Discussion** topics. In the chapters up to this point I have attempted to answer the questions I pose, and to properly explore the areas in which I trespass. In **Discussion** I am much more interested in posing questions without providing answers. I hope that you'll find material here which you can use as a springboard for further exploration with friends, colleagues and, of course, eager submissives.

Using control is often a case of combining experience, talent, skill, understanding and instinct.

When you lack understanding, then adapting your skills to new situations and partners is a hit-and-miss affair[2], simply because you don't know what is going on, and hence have no idea of how to fix it. In fact, much of life can become very interesting indeed if you don't really know what you're doing, and are just relying on things that have worked before... and then something changes.

To my mind, part of the challenge in life comes from understanding and dealing with demanding and unusual situations. Regardless of whether you are looking for challenges or not, it's certain that the less understanding you have, the more you are confined to standard solutions, and the less you are able to deal with non-standard problems. This book is about teaching you awareness and understanding so that you can see more solutions, and are confined less to standard problems.

I end this section noting that this book is mainly written for dominants. As they are the ones in control, they are the ones best placed to effect change... one would expect, anyway.

Note: because I'll be using "dominance & submission" to identify the activity, and the same words as two separate things, i.e. dominance on one hand, and submission on the other, I'll use an "&" between them when I'm talking about the activity, and an "and" between them if I happen to be talking about them as two separate things which just happen to be mentioned in the same sentence.

---

[2]Pun intended. Maybe I should have said "trial and error"?

1.1 What do you mean by dominance & submission?

It seems to me that there is, if not confusion, then at least a great deal of latitude in the use of labels in BDSM. There are *tops & bottoms*, *dominants & submissives*, *masters & slaves* and *mistresses & slaves*, and what each of these mean can significantly change, or even overlap, depending on which geographical region you're in, or to which community you belong. For example, what one person might refer to as a master & slave relationship, might be referred to by someone else as topping & bottoming.

Now, because there is this wide variation, I would like to talk about definitions for a few paragraphs to make my own meanings clear. My apologies to those whose own understanding of the terms does not align with mine.

I tend to think of *tops & bottoms* as people who mainly use sensation. It's true that the person wielding the flogger or tying the ropes is in control of the impact that the bottom feels, or is in control of the degree of physical freedom which the bottom has, but this is mainly because they have to create the situation or experience which allows the bottom to go where they need or want to go in their mind. There isn't much exploration of personal control; and it's mainly about two people doing something together physically, but going separate ways mentally and spiritually. Also, as a generality, the activities of tops and bottoms are confined to well-defined scenes. These scenes have a clear start and a clear end.

In some locales, what I've just described as *tops & bottoms* would be what people call *dominants & submissives*. I would agree that sometimes dominants and submissives do the same activities as tops and bottoms—and even sometimes get the same pleasures and satisfactions from them, but I see dominants and submissives as having a commitment to exploring control with each other which often extends beyond the end of any planned scenes. Dominance & submission is usually not something that they do as a scene, and from which they then simply walk away. Instead it's something that is part of their relationship. While the dominant partner might be able to go out and be submissive with someone else, or vice versa, within their relationship(s) they don't "switch" with each other. The dynamic stays—even if not apparent or active—with the one partner dominant and the other partner submissive all the time. Dominant & submissive relationships therefore have a long-term element.

Dominants and submissives explore control. I've used the term *control-sensitive* already, and here is where it gets important. For tops and bottoms, control is a tool to reach the state-of-mind or arousal that they are looking for. For dominants and submissives, control is not a tool but is the goal itself—feeling it, awareness of it as it ebbs and flows, taking it and giving it, deepening of it, and using it.

I think that the terms *masters & slaves* and *mistresses & slaves* are doomed to eternal confusion. Possibly because of the intensity historically and socially associated with the words, people seem to use them for practically any BDSM activity, even extending into just plain ol' fetishism where control plays no part at all.

My own take on *master (or mistress) & slave* is that they deal with control as a <u>need</u> where dominants and submissives might deal with control simply as a <u>want</u>. Well... that's what I like to think the terms mean but, as I say, they vary in meaning enormously depending on the terrain. I won't be using master, mistress or slave in this book any more. Instead, I'll be staying with *dominant* and *submissive*, and using them to refer to those people whose primary interest is control, whether it be as a want or a need.

The archetype

One of the problems with trying to define people, as I have just done, is that no one person ever fits in the one basket. There are many aspects to each individual. You can't just say that someone is a doctor, for example, and think that is all there is. They probably do other things as well as doctoring, maybe being a member of an amateur choir, or a chess player, or even a lover. They aren't just a doctor.

The same goes for tops, bottoms, dominants, submissives, masters, mistresses and slaves. A dominant might like doing "toppy" things from time to time, for instance, or a submissive might occasionally like tying up a friend. This makes them no less dominant or submissive.

What I was really doing with my definitions a few paragraphs ago, was defining *archetypes*. Something like taking an individual and removing all the bits that aren't, for example, dominant, and pointing to what remains and saying, "This is a dominant". Or, if you aren't keen on evisceration, what I was doing was focussing on the actual defining characteristics of each and ignoring characteristics which I see as secondary.

Conclusion

I certainly don't set myself up as the final word on definitions, but to understand where I'm coming from in this book, you need to accept that according to Peter Masters, a dominant is someone who seeks simply to take and use control over a submissive. A submissive seeks to give up control and to be controlled by a dominant.

Control is the key.

Things to think about

1. Why haven't I talked about love?
2. Why haven't I talked about sex?

1.2 Conscious, subconscious and unconscious

You can safely say that your submissive never ever reacts to you on a purely reasonable and rational basis. Everything they do and feel is going to be affected by previous experience with you and with others, various hungers and needs, social conditioning, and many other things, most of which they aren't aware of at the time. It's not just your submissive who is like this. They all are.

Just because you consciously and rationally take control of your submissive doesn't mean that there isn't going to be some deep down fear or resistance in them, or that there isn't some other part of their mind which's going to make the ride less than smooth. In this section I want to split the mind up into three levels—the *conscious*, *subconscious* and *unconscious*—and look at the characteristics of each and how each can either support or resist your attempts at control.

Conscious

The first, and the most obvious level, is the *conscious*. I say "obvious", because this is the place where we experience ourselves and our own personalities. It's in front of us all the time. It is the level of awareness, considered reactions, analysis and rational thought. It is where we think, feel and remember. This is also where we find our remember-able memories.

Not all memories can be remembered in the form in which

they occurred. There are also memories which we can no longer remember, i.e. those that have sunk into the subconscious, and whose effects continue to shape our thoughts and behaviours, such as when we're afraid of something but don't know why.

We rationalise and make decisions on the conscious level. We often use things that we know to help us make these decisions, rather than just purely react to the circumstances. Some examples:

1. You might be looking for a certain reaction from your submissive and use knowledge gained from previous experience with them to plan a way of getting it,

2. If you are a submissive, you might consciously decide to resist the attentions of a dominant because you know from talking to others that this particular dominant doesn't do things you like, or that they are not looking for the same sort of relationship you are,

3. At work you might have a knotty problem that takes all your knowledge and training to unravel,

4. If you are a dominant, you might choose a submissive to play with based on their attractiveness, your knowledge of what they're capable of, and your own awareness of what you think you're needing at the moment.

Our conscious choices and decisions are often coloured by influences which rise up from the subconscious and unconscious levels. Fear is an example of one such.

We might also have premonitions, experience "niggly" feelings about something, or act on our intuition. All of which are basically things which we've learned through experience and then subconsciously applied. All of these are non-conscious and, because there's nothing logical that we can grasp to justify them, they lack rationality. Even though they aren't rational in themselves, we can and do still use them in our equations when deciding what to do in many situations.

One characteristic you can use to help you recognsise if something is conscious or not is if it requires planning. Be aware though, that initially forming a plan to solve a problem is conscious, but replaying the same plan over and over again can just be a habit.

Subconscious

The *subconscious* is the home of training and conditioning, and is where memories, habits, and old feelings go once the conscious lets go of them. This is generally beyond the reach of conscious awareness. What is in the subconscious though, is still quite capable of influencing our choices and actions.

Forgotten or repressed memories are located in the subconscious. Once upon a time, of course, they were conscious—they were things that we experienced in some way—but, for some reason—be it because they weren't particularly interesting, or because they were too shocking, frightening, embarrassing or humiliating—we "allowed" them to be forgotten. The only difficulty with this, is that nothing can be completely forgotten. Every single thing that happens to us makes its mark on our minds and, even if we consciously cannot recall it, it will still influence us to some—possibly minor or possibly major—extent.

Habits are located in the subconscious. Sometimes we are aware of our habits—like smoking, biting nails, certain ways of speaking, favourite lunchtime haunts, etc. There are many more habits of which we are totally unaware—like facial expressions we use when talking, ways we walk which reflect our feelings, physical attitudes we adopt towards other people, ways of thinking, convenient mental attitudes we adopt when dealing with problems, etc.

Habits of which we are unaware have unhindered influence over us. This is not necessarily a bad thing. Safe driving habits are a good thing to have, and when we have them, we use them without even realising it. On the other hand, a habit of jumping to conclusions is a bad thing, and we might also do that without realising it.

Our habits are influences upon our actions. Many habits are good—like the aforementioned safe driving habits, or always looking both ways when we cross the street—and we encourage their development. Some habits of course, might not be so good. All habits of which we are consciously aware are modifiable. That is to say, we can consciously override or modify them—stop them, delay them, change them in some detail—like walk a different way to work, or put off the morning cup of coffee until later.

It is worth considering that nature (human or otherwise), in her parsimony—and man, in his incessant quest for finding easier ways of doing things, will generally not allow a habit to continue to exist which does not serve some profitable purpose, however dubious it might seem. This means that good habits and bad habits exist for a reason.

Smoking, as an example of a bad habit, has—in common with worry beads, nail-biting and doodling—the redeeming feature of giving the victim something to do with their hands and, hence, discharging some nervous energy.

It is the nature of the subconscious to be fairly mechanical and unimaginative. It is therefore the appropriate place to locate something like good driving skills, because from here they will be mechanically applied with a minimum of supervision from the conscious. A reward of this sort of habit is that it frees the conscious to perform other tasks, like problem solving or having a conversation.

While we may actively participate in the creation of some habits—for example, the now-famous good driving habits—they become activities with a life of their own. They are, as I said, modifiable by conscious choice, but can become so deeply ingrained that overriding them or cancelling them can be extremely difficult. If you have ever travelled overseas and had to drive on the other side of the road, then you'll know how difficult it is and how watchful you must be over yourself, i.e. over your own subconscious.

We don't have any first-hand experience of what goes on in the subconscious. By definition it contains things that are mostly inaccessible or lost to conscious awareness. We can only guess at what's in it by observation.

In engineering terms, we might consider the subconscious to be a *black box*—generally, "any automatic apparatus performing intricate functions" (from the Oxford English Dictionary), where what actually happens inside the box is unknown and can only be determined or guessed at by looking firstly at what goes in, and then at what comes out, and then analysing what has gone on between times.

This means that it might be the case that we wonder why we feel a certain way about something, but our original memories of what happened and how we felt at the time are vague or non-existent. It might be that the forgotten memories of this personal experience still linger in the subconscious, or it might be that our subconscious learned something from that experience. Whatever the cause, the subconscious brings its own influence to bear on our conscious whenever we encounter that same *something* again.

To learn about these subconscious reactions to things, it's necessary to explore related memories, observe our reactions and feelings, collect as much information as possible, and then try to divine what's inside this particular black box (e.g ourselves or our partners).

It's important to be aware that what arrives in our conscious from the subconscious is only an influence or suggestion as to how the subconscious would have us react. It typically isn't an absolute imperative or overwhelming compulsion, and with a bit of determination we can either ignore, modify or override it. The strength of the subconscious' influence is dependent on the impact of the original experiences and how quickly this impact decays.

How quickly the influence of a subconscious memory decays—i.e. how quickly it loses its potency over time—depends on many things: if and when it is reinforced, whether other things happen which create counter-influences, conscious effort to defeat the influence, the relevance of the influence to the changing lifestyle and physical and mental capabilities of the individual, etc.

It is very important to be aware that many of the personal experiences which leave their mark on our subconscious are not traumatic. Many of the things which shape our subconscious come from our environment—from the behaviour of family, friends, peers and from others in all the rest of our society. This general shaping influence is what directs our energies and inclinations towards activities and ideas of which our micro- and macro-societies "approve". They are, behaviourally speaking, *positively reinforced.*

Training and conditioning also exist in the subconscious. When you train, or are trained, in any activity—be it sport, service, mental skills or anything else—the regular and mechanical skills which you learn, physical or mental, take up residence in the subconscious.

Conditioning is similar. It is a process where some stimulus or trigger is made to produce a reaction it would not normally produce. This is done by repetitively pairing it with a stimulus which does produce the desired reaction. Pavlov's famous dogs are an example of this, where a bell was rung each time the dogs were given food. Eventually the dogs would salivate when they heard the bell, even when they weren't given food.

The key to both training and conditioning is repetition.

And, while on the subject of repetition and the subconscious, *advertising* can incline its victims towards the subconscious belief that by smoking (or by owning a particular model of car, or by drinking a particular brand of alcohol, etc.) they will soon be surrounded by attractive members of the opposite sex, be the centre of attention at parties, and always be fashionably dressed.

From the point of view of control here are some examples of how the subconscious can be an influence:

1. If your submissive has been previously conditioned by someone to respond in certain ways, you can initially take control by using the same triggers,

2. You can also use this previous conditioning as a starting point for new conditioning,

3. Previous bad experience with a dominant with some similarity to you—either the way they looked or behaved—can cause your submissive to subconsciously resist you, even though they might be consciously aware that there's no relationship between you and the previous dominant,

4. Your submissive's previous positive experience with being controlled in certain situations or environments (like while on a leash), can make them more likely to respond positively in the same situation with you.

Unconscious

The *unconscious* is the part of the mind shaped by evolution. It is the collection of predispositions and instincts which lets us each be and act as the human animals we are, and to survive as a species. In many ways it is the primal side of our natures.

We have some simple instincts, like our reaction to pain where we automatically pull our hand away from something hot. Fear of strangers is more complex and less obvious, but logical when you consider it as a survival instinct. The instinctive sex drive is also logical from a survival point of view, and interesting because of the fact that it develops only after a certain age, showing that we are programmed to develop physical and emotional characteristics and behaviours at certain times of life.

Even some basic personality types are built-in—Warrior and Hero, Mother, Father/Protector and Children being a small subset. For example, all mothers have a tendency to behave in similar ways towards their children, just as all children have a tendency to behave in similar ways towards their mothers. These built-in behaviours pre-equip us for situations which we will encounter when dealing with life in general.

Of course, a Warrior is just a normal man until something happens (e.g. a threat) which triggers the Warrior in him. In the same way, a Mother is just a woman until something happens—a child appears, or a member of the family becomes sick—which triggers the Mother-nurturer predisposition. Although some predispositions—like the two I just mentioned—are typically associated with a particular gender, that doesn't mean that they don't exist in the opposite gender. It's likely that the basic ones exist in all of us, but that some are usually easier to arouse in individuals of one gender than the other. So, for example, it's usually easier to arouse the Warrior or Fighter in a man than in a woman.

I'll be looking more closely at these in the upcoming section on **Predispositions**.

A way we can tell that these and other predispositions towards certain behaviours are "built-in" instead of learned, is that they appear as common motifs throughout ranges of unconnected cultures and histories.

As with the subconscious, we don't have any first-hand experience of the unconscious. It is even harder to work out what goes on in the unconscious because its influence is typically "coloured" or altered by the subconscious before it reaches our conscious minds. We also don't have the advantage of any memories, however vague, of what went into it to form it. In the case of the subconscious, we might be able to remember at least the form of many of the experiences from our past that contributed to the shaping of our subconscious. With the unconscious we don't have that.

The unconscious is not personal. Its nature isn't determined by our own personal experiences and history as is the subconscious. It is determined instead by the experiences of our species over the millions of years it has taken to develop. It contains instincts and inclinations towards certain behaviour that have helped our ancestors survive. Genetic variation ensures that the combinations and strengths of each of the instincts and inclinations—such as hunting ability, hand-eye coordination, intelligence, dominance, physical strength, athletic ability, ability to recognise patterns, etc.—is different for each individual. The unconscious is the foundation upon which the whole personality is built, and the variation between individuals ensures a wide variety of personality types.

Here are some ways in which the unconscious gets involved in control:

1. As you're probably aware, sex drive, and hormones rushing hither and thither in the body, can have a major impact on decision-making. Sex is also something that has a large instinctive component for us humans. Physically manipulating someone's sex drive—turning them on or off sexually via sexual presentation, touching or smell—is a good way to influence or direct their actions and choices,

2. Pain is also a strong influence at the unconscious level, and you can easily use it to physically control or position someone,

3. There are unconscious predispositions towards dominance and submission (which I'll be talking more about later

in the book). By using triggers that the unconscious recognises—e.g. physical force—you can trigger an unconscious submissive response.

Inter-communication

Communication between individuals generally works level-to-corresponding-level. That is, the conscious of one person "speaks" to the conscious of the other, the subconscious of one "speaks" to the subconscious of the other, and the unconscious "speaks" to the unconscious of the other. Each level knows the "language" which the same level in the other person understands.

It's important to realise that this means that each level uses a different language—a different set of actions or gestures, for example—from the others. Using the wrong language can mean that the message you are sending out just isn't received.

For example, speaking rationally and logically to someone in the grip of subconscious fear is not going to make a lot of difference to what they are experiencing. Likewise, communicating your feelings of sexual hunger to someone in any other way than through physical contact is probably not going to work very well either.

The different levels communicate with words, tone of voice, actions, attitudes, postures, smells, touch, gestures and so on. At any particular time, all the levels are communicating in some way. It's your job to look, hear and feel what they are all saying.

Conclusion

What I've tried to do in this section is draw your attention to three separate origins of behaviour or thought in both you and your submissive. These are:

- Conscious and considered thought and behaviour,

- Subconscious learned behaviour and conditioning, and
- Instinctive unconscious behaviour and reactions.

Each of these is accessible to you in some way. Each communicates in its own way.

Taking control can mean more than just directing your submissive rationally and logically; it can also mean learning the nature of their subconscious and unconscious, and asserting your control in actions and words that these levels understand, and to which these levels respond.

Things to think about

1. Draw up three lists, one for each of the conscious, subconscious and unconscious. List the things that your submissive does, the reactions they have, and work out from which level of the mind they are coming from.

2. Which levels of your submissive's mind interest you the most? What do you do to assert your control there?

1.3 Predispositions

Even before we leave the womb we already have inclinations, biases or predispositions towards certain attitudes, behaviours, thoughts and skills due to the structure of our brains. These are predispositions only, and not all of them are going to ever appear. Whether a particular one ever does show up is going to depend on how strong it is, whether there are any stronger competing predispositions, opportunity and any social or other conditioning which either supports or suppresses that predisposition.

For example, up until relatively recently in western society, women were completely discouraged from academia, engineering or science. Regardless of any individual woman's predisposition or innate ability, the social conditioning of either her, or the people around her, prevented her from expressing this. For a very long time, only very few women were able to break through this barrier—women like Hildegard Von Bingen, Ada Lovelace and Mary Shelley.

As a further example, we could consider a man who has the innate cunning and coordination to be a good hunter. If he is born into a modern lower social class he might never have the opportunity or encouragement to become a hunter, regardless of whether it is a hunter of animals for food, a corporate raider or some other type of hunter. In his own way though, if this predisposition is strong enough it will appear anyway, possibly in his choice of sports.

Some predispositions are relatively passive. They're there, and they can be used or not. If they're not used, then it's no big deal. These might be simple inclinations towards certain skills, such as having an analytical mind, or having good hand-eye coordination. These are generally useful in a wide range of activities.

Then there are other predispositions which are much more active and focussed. They make themselves known right from birth, like a naturally curious mind. There is a <u>drive</u> associated with them, as a result of which they push themselves forward and struggle for attention. They make it known that they are there and that they want out!

Some collections of these built-in predispositions can be so complex as to be more-or-less complete personalities. Carl Jung[3] called these *archetypes*, and, in fact, I wrote about these a little when talking about the unconscious earlier. In certain situations these can take over from the main personality. In these case, while you might see the same physical person and recognise similar behavioural quirks, when they are being driven by an archetype, their attitudes and biases are different to when they are being driven by another archetype, or when their main personality is active.

For example, when you are a hunter and you are actually out hunting, it means that for long periods of time you are functioning simply as a hunter. In the rest of your life, you might also be a mother or father, a business executive, home handyman or whatever, but for the duration of the hunt you are simply a hunter—the other aspects of you are suppressed. People who know you when you're not being a hunter could recognise you physically while you were hunting, but your behaviour might be completely new to them. Being just a hunter though, does not create what we would call a well-rounded individual, but in the right circumstances—i.e. during a hunt—being <u>only</u> a hunter is just right.

As another example, consider that a woman can turn into a mother right before your very eyes—like when her child is in-

---

[3] A famous early 20th century psychiatrist and contemporary of Sigmund Freud.

jured. She's still the same person, but clearly a new set of priorities, behaviours and attitudes have been turned on, and these basically amount to a nearly complete new personality.

Jung recognised and documented a number of archetypes, including the Mother[4], the Hero, and the Warrior. The fact that these are built-in is why they can come so naturally to us. The archetypes supply the basic attitudes or personality structures so that we don't have to learn them from scratch. We then change them or modify them to suit our particular needs—like to suit what we are hunting, our weapons, whether we are hunting alone and so on. The archetypal Mother might be modified to suit the number of children, what their needs are at the time (are they hungry, or are they sick?), the resources available in the community—such as play areas, friends—and so on. The basic archetypes remain the same, but we massage them into slightly new shapes to suit the needs of the time.

So, unconscious predispositions can range from simple skills and abilities through to nearly complete personalities. Being unconscious means that they are universal to all human minds. How can we be sure of this? How can we be sure that some of them aren't learned at an early age?

One way—used by Jung—was to look at mythologies from a range of different cultures and times. Jung reasoned that similar themes, personality-types and stories appearing in all cultures—especially those with no contact with other cultures—had to be archetypal. They resonate across all cultures and all times regardless of the social situations. These myths were moulded and

---

[4]I've been using the Mother as an example a fair bit here, and it might be useful to explicitly list some of the common behaviours in all mothers like nurturing, making physical contact, looking after the child when it's sick, cleaning and physically taking care of the child, protecting the child, teaching the child, finding food for the child, making the child fend for itself once it's old enough, and so on. Not all mothers have the same priorities, but the Mother archetype provides a core set of behaviours on which the real mother can draw—sort of ready-to-wear attitudes and behaviours.

propagated by generations of story-tellers, written and rewritten by generations of scribes, and all the while the components of the mythologies that resonated with each story-teller were reinforced and the individual fantasies of individual story-tellers were filtered out thus leaving an archetypal core.

Control

What does this all have to do with taking control? The answer is that archetypes give us access to the unconscious, and if we're looking to control someone we need to look for control, not just at the conscious level, but also at the unconscious and subconscious levels. Recognising the predispositions and archetypes present in a submissive lets you:

1. Better come up with strategies and techniques to take full advantage of the submissive, and
2. Better develop strategies to deal with things that might resist you (e.g. a dominant or independent streak in your submissive, or a subconscious fear).

Looking at myths, you can not only see particular personality types (e.g. the Hero), but also particular behaviours and attitudes. For example, good Kings are almost invariably dominant and assertive, and Heroes, while mostly dominant and assertive, are submissive to the will of their King (typically kneeling unhesitatingly before, accepting the orders of, and serving their king.)

Women in myths are, in general, submissive to the will of the strong men in their lives, and these same men usually don't hesitate to assert themselves. It would seem then, that dominance and submission are archetypal. And we've seen that things which are archetypal can be triggered or manipulated.

It's worth keeping in mind while considering all this, that myths tend to be filtered and strengthened by the tellers. The raw stuff of life, the predispositions, instincts and archetypes, are all amplified and presented in an extreme form. On the other hand, there are few myths regarding grocery shopping, or cleaning the kitchen floor, or going to visit sick relatives. These activities just don't trigger anything inside us—they don't activate hungers or inspire passions.

Manipulating archetypes

Archetypes, the unconscious or instinctive personalities about which I've been talking, don't typically respond just to particular physical situations. Instead, they mainly respond to other archetypal personalities. The Mother responds to the archetypal Child, to the basic characteristics and behaviours that all children have. It's not enough to simply be a small person to trigger the Mother archetype; the shape of the eyes, the behaviour and the sounds that a Child make all go together to trigger the Mother.

Heroes respond to Damsels-In-Distress (amongst other things), as distinct from any other women who happen to be passing by, and Warriors respond to the Adversary as opposed to just some guy standing around minding his own business.

Archetypes in other people can be controlled or influenced. By understanding the archetype which you want to be active, and how you want it to react, you can consciously perform the actions that will trigger or un-trigger it. For instance, physically lowering yourself and making yourself seem smaller can disarm the Warrior, or physically rising up above a non-Warrior can trigger submission.

Keep in mind though, that this is an exercise in communication, and that at the same time you are consciously expressing yourself, your subconscious and unconscious will also be expressing themselves by means of facial expressions, gestures, and inflections in your voice of which you are usually unaware[5]. To

---

[5] I talk much more about this in the chapter on **Communication** (page 99).

get the best effect in your listener, it pays to be aware of your own archetypes and how to trigger them, and then align them with the message you are trying to send. Your instinctive, unconscious and primal Dominant, for example, when active, will be communicating with the instinctive Submissive in your listener and can reinforce any dominating effect you are consciously trying to get across.

Societal archetypes and the subconscious

So far in this section I have been looking at universal, culture-independent archetypes and dispositions. These are useful because they give you an understanding which applies to everyone. However, you can also find things similar to these unconscious archetypes which occur just within a society or group. These are *societal archetypes* and they're caused by everyone within the group being exposed to, and conditioned by, the same things.

Collars, for example, fall into this category in BDSM circles, as do leather-clad, flogger-toting individuals who get recognised as dominants—and who trigger corresponding subconscious reactions in others... at least initially—regardless of what they really are, and regardless of their skill level. As members of the larger community we respond to uniforms (e.g. police officer or fire-brigade officer), to types of car, to business suits, to office decor and so on.

Images

To control subconscious or unconscious archetypes you have to know what they respond to or what triggers them. A trigger must have some combination of characteristics which we subconsciously or unconsciously recognise. Somewhere in the mind of each of us, for example, there must be an "image" of an archetypal Child. When a real child comes along which is a close-enough match to the archetypal child image, the Mother archetype will be triggered.

The same occurs with a Warrior. An Adversary must be perceived by the unconscious to trigger the Warrior. Thus, an image of the Adversary is also built-in to us. An archetype which is triggered in the wrong situation—like the Warrior if confronted with a Child—is waste of energy and is not a survival characteristic.

The image or images which trigger an archetype are not simply static visual images—like photographs or costumes—but instead can be, and often are, complete behaviours including actions, posture, facial expressions, tone of voice and so on, as well as appearance. It isn't enough, for example, to trigger the Mother archetype that something simply looks like a baby—it needs to act and move like a baby, be the same size as a baby, have the facial expressions of a baby and sound like a baby. Indeed, the intensity of the Mother archetype response isn't only dependent on the presence of a baby, but is modified by variations of the "baby" image—for example, baby-in-distress, hungry-baby, or baby-having-a-nap.

In the same way, if you want to trigger or manipulate a subconscious or unconscious Submissive archetype, then you also need to know the images to which it'll respond. By using these you reach past the conscious and rational mind of the individual and directly tweak and manipulate the Submissive at their core. This is how you can get a deep reaction. The closer the real-world trigger is to the archetypal trigger, the stronger the archetypal response.

Next I'd like to talk about some of the images to which we respond, and discuss their subconscious or unconscious origins.

Threat and aggression, dominance and submission

Most animals, at any significant stage of evolutionary development, respond to the physical size of other animals. When confronted by a member of the same or of a different species, animals—including humans—will determine the threat posed partly on the basis of the size of this other individual. This characteristic lends itself to manipulation and it's common for an animal—including a human—to "raise itself to its full height" in an attempt to intimidate a potential enemy. Some species can inflate or puff themselves up—as in the case of cats and some fish, for example—so as to appear bigger and hence more of a threat. Holding the arms, upper limbs or wings apart also works to make an individual physically larger and more threatening. Forward movements—i.e. towards the other individual—can be threatening. Backwards movements, on the other hand, are less threatening or even appeasing.

An intentional decreasing of size is often used to indicate submission or surrender to the strength of another. In herd species—such as lions, elephant and man—crouching down or lowering the head is such an indication. This sort of behaviour can often be symbolic, showing submission even before any threat or combat has occurred.

Eye contact can be an indication of readiness to fight. Deliberate lowering, or turning away, of the eyes is an indication that the individual does not want to fight and, indeed, is not prepared to fight or oppose.

In the human kingdom, height is an element of ritual in many cultures, including our own. Hats and various forms of headdress have been used since at least the beginning of recorded history to symbolically increase the perceived height of an individual[6]. Even the three-tiered podium where athletes receive their medals and formal acclamation is another such device.

On the other hand, lowering of the head—which also, coincidentally, removes eye contact—is often the minimum behaviour

---

[6]Consider a Pharaoh's headdress, american indians' high, feathered headdress, top hats worn by aristocracy in recent centuries, and headwear showing rank in churches (e.g. pope, bishop and cardinal.)

indicating respect for the rank or station of someone. Bowing down or kneeling—such as when receiving formal religious, political or royal recognition, such as a knighthood—is used to indicate extreme submission.

Dominance and submission aren't just involved in confrontation, threat and aggression, of course. Leadership and cooperative behaviour (teamwork), in all their forms, have elements of dominance and submission, too.

While it might be that some of the characteristics which are unconsciously associated with dominance, such as height or large physical size, are typically innate male characteristics, this doesn't mean that these and other characteristics can't be manipulated by anyone, including females, to produce similar effects in submissives. High-heeled shoes and padded shoulders for women can be examples of such manipulations.

Confidence and assertiveness when making decisions are things that can trigger submission, as can physically manipulating the submissive, by holding them by the hair or putting something around their neck, for example. Military or other service uniforms also tend to be effective. Tone of voice is important. Making and holding eye contact are also. Your physical attitude towards your submissive, whether you are physically very close or looking down on them are also triggers.

One very important characteristic of a dominant is the ease with which they accept submission. For someone with an innately and strongly active submissive nature, the acceptance of their submissiveness by a perceived dominant is an important trigger to release more of it.

Sexual attraction and arousal

Sexual arousal—which would include those stages of "interest" before any obvious signs of physical arousal, such as penile erection or vaginal lubrication—is partly unconscious. It is clearly a survival characteristic that we automatically recognise and respond to an appropriately-equipped member of our same species. Sexually responding to a tree, while it may have certain phallic symbolism, is likely not to be appropriate or rewarding. On the other hand sexually responding to a physically mature and youthful individual stands a real chance of being a good thing in the keeping-the-species-going department. Thus it is likely that each of us has built-in "images" of both how a sexually attractive male and a sexually attractive female should be.

The penis, even when erect, is fairly small in the grand scheme of things. Vaginas also are often hard to discriminate. What we most likely respond to are physical body size, size of hips—both in men and women, length of hair[7], firm and round breasts[8], indications of physical fitness and lack of deformity, and behaviour indicating that they are attracted to us[9].

We will also respond to other characteristics indicative of gender including:

1. Way of walking[10],

---

[7]Men, in their archetypal role as hunter, and based on observations of existing primitive tribes, might typically have had short hair. This doesn't mean though, that hair length is a strong component of the archetypal image of a sexually attractive female. In our own western society it is very likely that societal images (and the ubiquitous advertising) are the main determinants for our own fascination with long, straight hair in women.

[8]Small breasts might indicate sexual immaturity, and floppy or low-hanging breasts might indicate a woman who already is bonded to another man, or indicate one who is beyond a useful age for breeding (i.e. old).
Weirdly, one common breast image, at least in advertising, is knees. It's common to see close-up photographs of young women with their knees drawn up to their chest. While the women may be fully dressed, with their knees up close to their chests, the right curves seem to be showing in the right geographical location, sufficient to trigger a response (even if it's just a second glance, at which point you realise that the curves you're seeing are actually the woman's round kneecaps).

[9]For example, eye contact, smiles, sexual presentation (such as uncrossing arms and pushing forward breasts, chest or hips), etc.

[10]E.g. women's wider hips often cause a different gait to that of a man.

2. Any nurturing behaviour,

3. Aggressiveness or assertiveness,

4. Submissiveness.

While it's also built-in that we respond when we see these characteristics, this inclination is significantly modified by influences coming from the subconscious. Previous experience with friends, colleagues, teachers, parents, and with siblings, will shape our sexual preferences in various ways—both by giving us characteristics which we will tend to avoid when selecting a sexual partner, and other characteristics which we will tend more to seek. The extent to which the unconscious sexual predispositions are modified by the subconscious will vary from individual to individual, depending on their experiences and their own self-awareness.

Images presented to us by our micro- or macro-societies will also heavily condition us. An interesting example of this is that we, in our own western society, are largely conditioned to sexually respond to people who titillatingly reveal small amounts of chest or breast, regardless of the fact that we can often see much more at the beach; and that in other, more "primitive", societies, most people spend most of their public lives walking around in near nakedness with interesting bits hanging out everywhere.

Sources of this subconscious conditioning are sometimes easy to identify. Advertising is always a good candidate to consider as its explicit goal is to deliberately manipulate our behaviour. Religion, in the case of sexual behaviour, is another good candidate.

A couple of other obvious sexual images are worth mentioning before finishing this sub-topic. Phallus-shaped objects are common enough, and phallus-shaped dildos and vibrators are wide-spread[11]. Red, wet (glossy) lips are also a common image, both on the street and in movies, TV and advertising, and their symbolic similarity with aroused vaginal lips is well known.

---

[11] No pun intended... or maybe it was.

More than one photographer has used the profile image of a firm red lipstick approaching already-glossy red female lips, and at least one version of this style of photo has appeared where the tip of the lipstick was shaped to clearly represent the head of an erect penis. The sexual symbolism is clear, and it is designed to trigger both subconscious and archetypal sexual responses in us.

Calling forth an archetype

I suppose, in a way, I might have given the impression here that taking control via archetypes and predispositions involves a certain amount of faking so as to trigger a reaction in your submissive.

This could be a way of doing it, but the best way for you to get a submissive reaction from your submissive is to draw on your own dominance. Just as the archetypal Mother is tuned to the archetypal Child, so the archetypal Submissive is tuned to the archetypal Dominant. Drawing on your own archetypal Dominant is the key, both to getting a better and stronger reaction from your submissive, and to getting a better and more satisfying response from yourself.

So how do you do it?

Well, just as you need to learn what triggers work on your submissive, you also need to learn what triggers you. Do you feel more dominant after you've seen a Claude Van Damme or Arnold Schwarzenegger movie, or after you've seen Sigourney Weaver kick butt in one of the Alien movies? Do your dominant juices start to flow when you grasp the neck of your submissive and see them melt to their knees in front of you? Does pulling on your leather gear do it for you? Or does pulling yourself up to your full height and experiencing yourself towering over your submissive trigger you?

You could just wait for the right muse to strike you, but taking control also means taking control of yourself. Learn about yourself and what drives you so that you can use your own feelings and archetypes to drive your submissive.

Conclusion

Awareness and understanding of unconscious and subconscious archetypes, and of predispositions, give us *hooks* with which we can manipulate and control. Some hooks work better than others, of course, and some people will be more or less responsive than others. These hooks do though give us a good starting point, and their existence means that there are things we can do with some confidence that they will be successful most of the time.

Our increased understanding of these hooks also makes it easier for us to recognise when someone is attempting to manipulate or control us via these same archetypes.

Things to think about

1. What triggers a dominant "rush" in you? What fires it up? Is it sexual? Is it related to some other activity? Is it related to images you see? Are there things completely unrelated to your submissive which trigger you?

2. If you're submissive, what is it that triggers you? Are there images or actions which do it for you?

3. On the other hand are there things that specifically turn you off? When you're feeling particularly dominant or submissive, are there things that will put you straight back into neutral?

1.4 Evolution

Layers

We are the current end-of-the-line of millions of years of evolution. An interesting thing about this is that, just as our physical appearance and capabilities are evolved from our primate ancestors, and that their appearance and capabilities were evolved from their ancestors and so on back to the beginning of life, so too our brains and many aspects of our behaviour are evolved from those of the primates and so on back to the beginning of life.

The earliest clusters of neurones—the precursors of the brain—came into being to regulate the operation of different simple functions of the body—breathing and heart rate for example.

Later evolution produced instincts and predispositions towards particular behaviours which increased the likelihood of survival of both the individual and the species. These include things such as cooperative behaviour, hunting instincts, parenting instincts, mating instincts and so on.

An important thing to understand, is that all this developed largely in layers. The oldest surviving behaviours exist on the inside of our brains and minds with later-developing behaviours and structures being layered over the top of these. Often this is very apparent physically in the actual structure of the brain, and through the comparison of human brains to lower animals... but this is getting off-topic and I'll leave further exploration of this aspect to the reader.

Two consequences of all of this evolution are:

1. That the older behaviours and structures are often the strongest and more mature, and,

2. They are often furthest away from the influence of the late-developing conscious or self-aware mind.

As a result, while many instincts and behaviours can be partially or completely overridden by conscious effort, there are many which are very resistant to conscious control (e.g. heart beat, hunger for food, thirst, reactions to pain, and sexual arousal).

You should also note that while for clarity I have been giving examples of physical functions to highlight the nature of evolutionary development, much more importantly—at least for the subject of this book—are the attitudes, emotions and intellectual behaviours which have also evolved in the same way and over the same period of time.

As we wander about the subject of control you'll see that the consideration of where an instinct or behaviour comes from is often particularly relevant when you are trying to work out how to control or direct it.

Cooperation and dominance & submission

It's a nice idea that everyone should be equal, but any gathering of two or more individuals needs them each to take different roles. Even a group of just two people going to the movies needs someone to actually make up the collective mind, once suggestions have been made as to what they're going to see.

This sort of cooperative behaviour is built in to us, and is common in other animals, even the very primitive. You can see it in the way ants don't all struggle to carry the same grain of food, but manage to have just enough ants doing the job while the other ants forage for other food; and in the way bees communicate and work together to get the best amount of pollen; and in the way herds of larger animals actually manage to stay and work together—with some individuals foraging for food, some taking care of the young, and some performing guard duties (e.g. in elephant herds)—rather than all struggle along as individuals.

We humans live as family units within larger social groups or herds. This is part of our evolutionary heritage, and as part of this we each have other predispositions towards certain behaviours and roles which lubricate this.

The alpha male, or the pack or herd leader, is common enough in our own human world, both in primitive tribes and modern society. A consequence of the existence of alpha males or dominant individuals in a group or society, is that for such members of the group to be effective, a large proportion of the rest of the group must have submissive behaviours. I don't mean "submissive" necessarily in a BDSM sense, but instead in the sense that the group needs to readily accept the choices and the direction of the dominant members. The group really does need to work together, rather than as a thousand individual kings, and this means acceptance of direction from the minority by the majority.

I would argue then, that there is an evolutionary basis for the existence of behaviour of an enduring, submissive or accepting nature. If so, it's likely that we each are also pre-wired with a predisposition both towards dominant behaviour and towards submissive behaviour, and that each comes out in the appropriate circumstances. The appropriate circumstances are going to depend on what we perceive to be needed—consciously, subconsciously and/or unconsciously—in the current situation, and on our reaction to the other people present at the time. We have carried a lot of this pre-wiring with us through much of our evolution, and it is likely to be fairly old, and hence very strong, in evolutionary terms.

Variation

Just how dominant or submissive each individual is, and how readily their dominance or submission manifests itself, will depend partially on genetic variation, as well as on cultural and family influences. We don't all look the same, though we share similar characteristics (like two legs, a heart, two eyes, and a taste for hamburgers), and we don't all have the same physical and mental characteristics from birth. This is genetic variation, and it serves to make each of us better adapted to a different range of situations, activities, occupations and roles.

As part of this, some people are going to be inherently more inclined towards choosing a dominant role, while others will be biased towards choosing a submissive role. I suspect, on the basis of observation, physical size, and on the way our recent evolutionary ancestors behave, that there will also be more of a bias towards dominance among men than women. This doesn't mean that men are the only ones going to be dominant, but instead that there's a higher possibility of dominance being associated with being male than female. This tendency towards dominance will also vary in any particular individual according to the situation in which they find themselves.

Situation

The situations in which individuals and groups find themselves will affect the likelihood and extent to which dominance and submission are triggered in each person. How much each individual is triggered, and in what way, will depend to some extent on the circumstances. Below are some situations in which different individuals are likely to be triggered differently. As an exercise, consider how dominant, aggressive, decisive or outspoken you would be in each.

1. Large or public social gatherings with friends,

2. Small, intimate and private gatherings with friends,

3. Family groups or gatherings,

4. Situations where children are present,

5. Situations where someone is sick,

6. Public situations where submissives are present,

7. Intimate or private situations where submissives are present,

8. Situations where no submissives are present,

9. A one-on-one encounter with a lone submissive,

10. Situations where diplomacy is required,

11. Situations of potential physical or verbal conflict,

12. Situations in which one individual's particular skill or talent is needed.

Pleasure

Mother nature (i.e. evolution) ensures that we behave in certain ways by making some behaviours pleasurable or rewarding. Eating and sex, for example, can be jolly good fun and so we tend to do them a lot.

But the functions that eating and sex perform—nutrition and breeding—have no direct need to be pleasurable. Even if food tasted abysmal, it would could still do its job. The purpose of eating is to provide our bodies with nutrients—carbohydrates, fat, proteins, vitamins, etc.—so that it can function. The fact that the foods which match the needs of our bodies at a particular time actually taste good—such as salty foods when we are running low on salt—has no relation at all to the effect they have on our bodies. Ditto for sex. In fact, most of the time, we use sex for something other than creating new BDSM enthusiasts.

However, by being wired so that eating and sex are pleasurable, evolution makes sure that we do them and thus survive as a species. In the same way, mother nature ensures that there will be people who can and will accept dominant roles, and that there will be others who will accept submissive roles, by making these behaviours pleasurable in themselves.

Indeed, in most social situations, it's necessary that there be some who impose their decisions on others, and others who accept these decisions. If we were all wired to be dominant all the time, there'd never be any consensus; and if were all wired to be submissive all the time, then there'd be no decisions anyway.

So, we need to be able to dominate and to submit at different times. Some of us do better at the dominating side, and some at the submitting. And mother nature can make sure that we do (mostly) dominate and submit at the right time by making dominance and submission pleasurable.

Because eating and sex can be pleasant and satisfying, and because we have the free time and resources, we have made them into recreations or pastimes... and we have done the same things with dominance and submission.

Away from the stress and roles required in the "real world", many couples adopt dominant and submissive behaviours or attitudes in their private relationships as a form of recreation, or way of unwinding, even if a lot of the time it's not so clearly recreational and it mostly occurs outside of the "realm" of BDSM[12].

---

[12]Which makes me wonder whether dominance and submission could be hunger in a similar way to hunger for food and sex, and whether recreational BDSM is actually just a type of feeding behaviour.

State changes

Our predisposition towards certain behaviours at certain times is not limited towards us having hungers or cravings—such as for sex or certain foods. It also extends to affecting our state of mind so that we can better deal with situations in which we find ourselves.

Being hungry, for example, tends to awaken our sense of smell and taste buds, and makes us hunt for food. After eating, we have a tendency to slow down and relax, which gives our food a chance to digest. Sex drive increases some aspects of our alertness, and bumps up our metabolism and heart rate, as well increasing levels of aggression in both genders. And physical damage and pain cause chemicals to be released into our bloodstream to help us deal with them.

In similar ways there are physical and mental changes associated with dominance and submission. Sub-space, slave-space and the occasionally-mentioned dom-space are obvious examples[13]. The mental adaptations which occur in a submissive, in response to the physical and mental demands of a dominant, make them better able to cope with and indeed, enjoy what happens to them. Submissives often become more accepting and pliant and, sometimes, less articulate and mentally less sophisticated in response to the increasing control of the dominant. This latter strongly suggests that when we talk of submission, we are dealing with the more primal, or less developed, aspects of the inner layers of the brain.

---

[13] These *spaces* are states of mind. Sub- and slave-space are often reactions to the attentions of a dominant. Exactly what they are and how they feel, varies wildly between individuals, but common characteristics are feelings of detachment, loss of complexity, "floating", and a closer connection to the individual's elemental nature.

Dom-space is a state of mind into which a dominant enters as they interact with a submissive. It is usually highly focussed on the submissive and their reactions. Loss of complexity is common here, too.

What's interesting about this is that sub-space is an adaptation—a way of making a necessary behaviour or attitude pleasurable—in the same way that dominance is an adaptation. And just as sex and eating are used by us for recreational purposes beyond their original evolutionary "intention", so too the pre-wired rewards of dominance and submission can be, and are, used for pleasure beyond just what is strictly needed for social cooperation.

Conclusion

Evolution is in the past, and you could argue its relevance to the more practical aspects of control, but considering the possible effect of evolution on our ability to control others, and to be controlled by others, gives us another aspect from which to view control.

And just the same as understanding any complex structure requires viewing it from as many angles as possible, so too understanding control requires looking at it from as many angles as possible.

In this section on evolution, one of the ideas I have presented is that of the structure of the brain and mind being built up in layers, each higher layer being built on the foundation of lower layers, with the lower layers being the more primitive and the higher layers the more sophisticated. Recognising which behaviours come from the higher layers, and which come from the lower layers, lets us better work out what sorts of triggers and activities we can use to control them.

Another idea I have talked about, is that of pleasure being mother nature's way of getting us to perform some action which we might not otherwise perform.

Things to think about

1. Why is dominance and submission play often sexually arousing?

Chapter 2

Control

My own focus, or interest, in BDSM is *control-sensitive relationships*. In other words, I like control. Not just being in control, but the awareness of control, the feel of control, and the ability to manipulate control itself.

One of the most important things for me is to understand what happens when I take control from someone: the steps involved, how it proceeds, what can go wrong, how to reinforce control, and how to give back control when I'm done. Basically I'm interested in anything that has to do with the transfer of control to or from someone.

In this chapter I want to begin the exploration of control by looking at what actually happens when you take control of someone, and what happens when they give up control to you. I'll look at the ideal case—when it all goes right—and the non-ideal cases where it can go wrong. I also want to consider factors which help, and factors which hinder a *transfer of control*, and things which you can do to move the balance in your favour.

Conclusion

Certainly there is an element of natural ability in being a dominant, but just as tradesmen and sportsmen are made better by study and awareness of the principles and rules of their craft, so too, dominants who combine natural ability with an understanding of the underlying aspects and principles of control and submission can reach heights unattainable by natural ability alone.

Things to think about

Before we start I'd like you to consider what the following words mean to you:

1. Authority,

2. Power,

3. Control.

2.1 The process

Let's cut to the quick here. There is no direct connection between you and another person. There is no way that you can reach into someone's brain and twiddle their neurons so that their arms and legs move the way you want, or so that they think what you want, and yet you can still have control over them. How so? How do you take control? How does someone give it up?

Consider the following very short example:

> *You are sitting alone in your office, doing some work, and a respected colleague comes in and says in a decisive voice, "Get up and come with me!" You react by standing up and following your colleague out the door.*

What has just happened? Here are two of the possibilities:

1. You listen to what he says, think about how busy you are, evaluate a million-and-one other things, and then make the decision to follow him on the chance that what he has in mind is more important than what you're doing,

2. You get up automatically and follow him out the door without thinking about it.

For us control-o-philiacs the second possibility is the most interesting, but before we look at that, I want to take a quick look at the first possibility so that I can use it for contrast.

In the first possibility you are in control and you stay in control. You consider what your colleague says, and make your own choice about what to do. That you actually do what he says doesn't take away from the fact that it's your choice to follow him. If you had decided that you had something better or more important to do, you wouldn't have followed him.

In the second possibility though, your colleague takes control and you give it up without thinking—you follow without thinking, without deciding to do so.

Someone else taking control of us like this happens frequently. This office scenario is one such example. It also happens in a restaurant when you're waiting for a table and a waiter comes up and says, "Follow me!", or when a friend shows up while you're in a café and tells you to, "Move over!", when they want to sit on the same bench next to you, or if you're helping a friend to work on their car and they say, "Hand me that wrench!" Mostly you do let others take this sort of control readily, trusting the waiter to lead you to a table, or the friend in the café to not to be wasting your time by getting you to move, and so on.

On the other hand, if a waiter in a restaurant told you instead, "Remove your clothes!", you probably wouldn't. Why would you automatically follow the waiter to a table when he tells you to, but not undress in the same situation?

Clearly it depends on the context. The control that we are prepared to give up depends on many factors, including where, when, and who is trying to take control.

What we are considering here are temporary *transfers of control*. In the examples I've given so far, we temporarily give up control to someone. I will better define *transfer of control* shortly, and explain it in detail, but roughly speaking it occurs between two people when the first person performs an action which causes the second person to enter into a state of mind where they will uncritically and automatically accept direction from the first person. At the same time, the first person enters a state of mind where they "know" that the second person will accept direction from them.

Strangely enough, we aren't just controlled by people. We also give up control to things. Traffic signals are a good example of this. When you're driving along and you come to a red light, you don't actually weigh up in your mind whether to stop or not, you just do. This isn't quite as simple as it sounds. In a way, you don't actually make the decision to stop—the traffic signal does it for you. It takes control. You simply know that you have to stop, and once you "know" this, it's then up to you to enact this decision as best you can by looking in the rear-view mirror, checking how close you are to the intersection, and then working out how best to safely stop.

Any transfer of control from one person to another requires a specific action. Control doesn't transfer of its own accord. You can't just be sitting in a room with someone else and suddenly they're in control. And just as it requires a specific action, such as the one from your colleague in the office example at the beginning of this section, to take control from you, it also requires a specific action on your part to take back control, i.e. to transfer the control back to you. This action could be as simple as making the decision to do so.

In this book I am mainly interested in contexts which are relevant and useful to control-sensitive people, people for whom the taking and using of control is not just temporary or incidental—as in the examples above—but for whom transfer of control is an experience to be explored, deepened and prolonged. My position is that in the right, and possibly rare, circumstances you can take control over any aspect of someone else... provided they give up that same control[1]. For the rest of this section I am going to be looking very closely at what happens when control is transferred from one person to another, such from a submissive to a

---

[1] Note that this may not always be conscious. It may be subconscious or unconscious instead.

dominant[2]. In particular:

1. The process, or steps, involved in a transfer of control, and
2. What can go wrong in a transfer.

The four steps

At a minimum, a transfer of control involves the steps given in the table below. There can be more, but these are the basic and required steps; others might get added to reinforce the process. The steps always occurs in the order shown, but don't always immediately follow each other. In other words there can be any amount of time between steps. The time between steps can even be effectively instantaneous.

Step	Submissive	Dominant
1	Offers control (page 52)	
2		Takes control (page 53)
3	Gives up control (page 54)	
4		Accepts and asserts control (page 55)

1. Control on offer

Just as in the example of you and the waiter earlier, you have to be ready to give up control for someone to be able to take it. If the waiter told you to follow him when you weren't in his restaurant, then the likelihood that you would do so is much lower than if you were in his restaurant.

In his restaurant though, by putting yourself in the queue for a table you are making the required change in your mental state

---

[2]Although I am focussing on the dominant/submissive case here, many of the principles and ideas are equally applicable to other, "vanilla", people.

yourself. You are preparing yourself to give up control. You expect to be taken in charge and directed to a table. In your own mind you are offering up that control to the waiter. In busy restaurants this control won't be taken up straight away. You will be left waiting until a table becomes available, all the while you are still in the state of mind where you can be directed by a waiter.

In a BDSM context, similar things happen at parties and social gatherings where optimistic submissives look for some attention, and are already predisposed to following the directions of a dominant. This doesn't mean that they aren't doing things, such as getting themselves drinks, or mingling and chatting to people. They aren't inert, and they haven't given up control yet—they are just *ready* to give up control. In this situation, trust in the dominant, previous experience and conditioning, environment and conflicting states of mind (e.g. worries), are all elements which make up the context which determines what control is on offer and to whom.

Some control is going to be on offer from all of us practically all the time. Most people, for example, will respond automatically to instructions from a police officer doing his duty, and I have already given the example of traffic signals. In both these cases the predisposition to give up control is there practically all the time.

You might consider then, that this first step in a transfer of control is more a pre-existing condition than a step in some cases. That is, rather than something occurring which causes the submissive to offer up control, that it might be something in their nature which causes control to be available for the taking in some or all circircumstances.

2. Taking control

Taking control requires an action by the person taking control. The clearer and less ambiguous it is, the better. Actions can be giving instructions, like "Follow me!", or can be more physical, such as a dominant taking a submissive by the arm or hair, or by pointing or making gestures, or even by taking control of the personal space of the submissive by, say, stroking their neck or hair, or by moving up close.

The dominant doesn't have to know that control is on offer from the submissive. He can just fling the action at the submissive, so to speak, optimistically hoping that they'll respond. Or the dominant may already be aware by the submissive's posture, attitude, the way they speak or previous experience, that control is available for taking.

The point here is that it requires a concrete action, and it needs to be particularly concrete to the submissive because this action needs to trigger the following step, the actual giving up of control, in the submissive. If the taking-control action is unclear, then the submissive may not respond or may respond ambiguously.

3. Giving up control

Here is the point where a significant change of mental state occurs in the submissive. This change is where the submissive's control passes away from them to the dominant. The submissive sees, experiences or becomes aware that the dominant is taking up the control they had on offer. The submissive surrenders it and, therefore, loses it. This doesn't need to be conscious. As I've already indicated, most transfers occur without us being aware, and can happen unconsciously, subconsciously or consciously. In "ideal" cases they will occur on all levels[3].

So, the submissive gives up control. One consequence of this state of mind is that the submissive can't exercise that control

---

[3] By "ideal", I mean that if the transfer of control occurs at the conscious, subconscious and unconscious levels at the same time, then there will be no conflict. If the transfer occurred at, say, the unconscious level and the conscious resisted then the effectiveness of the transfer is reduced.

again until:

1. They either take it back, or
2. It is given back to them.

It is as if a switch had been thrown in the submissive's mind.

4. Asserting or accepting control

This final step in the basic sequence is where a complementary change of mental state to that of the submissive occurs in the dominant. The dominant accepts that they have the control given up by the submissive. Again, this doesn't necessarily occur consciously, but typically does occur as a result of feedback they get from the submissive—seeing the submissive do as they were told, changes in facial expression or posture, or other signs. Again, this is like a switch—the dominant is either in control or they aren't; there is no in-between.

Power hit

The office example at the beginning of this section is fairly basic. The likelihood of this colleague being successful at getting you to follow him is limited and highly variable. Let's change the situation around a bit, move it out of the formal office environment, and make it a submissive who is sitting in the room, and you are the one who enters wanting them to get up and follow you. There are more ways of taking control than just telling someone what to do. Your chances of success are going to be increased by the more avenues of control-taking you explore.

For example, instead of just entering the room and saying, "Stand up!", you could step up close to the submissive—thereby taking control of their personal space, cup their chin in your hand and gently lift—thereby taking control of a part of their body, and then verbally direct them to stand up—thereby taking control of their choice of what they do. What you have here are three control-actions each serving to reinforce the others.

Whether you choose to do such a *power hit* of control-taking will depend on how available the submissive is. You'll need to decide whether such an aggressive approach is best, or whether a more gradual, one-step-at-time approach will work better. This will depend on the situation, and on what you're trying to achieve.

Additional steps

After the basic transfer has occurred you—as the dominant—might, and probably would, take further steps to reinforce the transfer. In a way, this is "bedding down" or settling both you and your submissive into these new states of mind. Talking about it with your submissive, verbally acknowledging the control you now have, giving them instructions, and further asserting control over them, all serve to reinforce and possibly expand the control for them, and their reactions to it will further reinforce it for you.

What can go wrong in a transfer

The four steps I've just been talking about are the ideal progression. Life isn't always ideal though, and sometimes a transfer of control will go wrong. As I said at the beginning of the chapter, there is no direct way to twiddle your submissive's neurones. You can't directly put them in the state of mind where they give up control. It might sound fatalistic, but the best you can do is create the right situations and mind set, give the right signals, and look for the expected response.

In a broad way, everything that can go wrong has to do with communication failures. Here are a few of examples:

1. The dominant thinks that some control is on offer, attempts to take it, and nothing happens or else the submissive rejects

the attempt,

2. Consider an optimistic submissive at a party. They are sitting around waiting for a dominant to come along and express interest in them. A dominant comes along and tells them to do something, maybe to stand up and move. The submissive might think that the dominant is taking control of them, and they (perhaps subconsciously) up control. The dominant instead, just wanted a better view of something that's happening and the submissive was blocking his view. He had no intention of taking control of the submissive. Eventually the dominant moves on without realising that the submissive has given up control to him. The submissive is left in a sort of control limbo,

3. Consider a dominant at a party. They see an interesting-looking submissive and go up to them, and test their responsiveness by telling thm to stand up. The submissive does so, and the dominant then believes that they've taken control of the submissive. The submissive, on the other hand, just thinks that the dominant wanted to get past and was being polite.

There are, of course, endless variations on these, plus many others. In the first case the dominant "read" the submissive and got it wrong. In the last two cases someone thinks they've been part of a transfer of control, and have entered into the new state of mind as if they had, but they are alone in this state and have to recover by taking back control or giving up control, respectively.

Conclusion

The process involved in the transfer of control from one person, a submissive, to another, a dominant is definable. Once defined, it becomes something that can be studied and, in particular instances—whether they've worked or not—can be analysed, compared to the model we now have, and refined. I know this sounds clinical, but a solid understanding of the principles is what lets us systematically work towards doing "it" better.

Things to think about

1. I haven't yet talked much about how time is involved in the transfer process. Where and when can time be important?

2. Can you write down a few concrete examples of the four-step process, maybe starting with the original office example at the beginning of this section, and identify each step?

3. I didn't give an exhaustive list of examples of what can go wrong in a transfer. Can you look back on some of your own problematic experiences, try to fit them into the four-step model and then work out at what stage they went awry?

4. What criteria would you use to decide what sort of control-taking action or actions you should begin with when you have a new submissive? Are there things that almost always work, or some which you use to get a "feel" for the submissive? Do you try a few subtle things before deciding how to go in for the kill? How do you decide when to go slowly?

2.2 Consolidating control

In the last section I talked about the *transfer of control* process and listed its four basic steps. The actions which the person taking control, the dominant, do are very quick, taking typically no more than a second or two. This means that the key or "meaty" part of the transfer can be over in a matter of seconds. What happens next?

In the short term, there comes a phase of *consolidation* or "bedding down" of the control. This consolidation consists of defining the boundaries of the control, of exploring and actually asserting control over the areas of behaviour which the dominant is interested in.

Let's consider the case where your initial control-taking action over your submissive was to direct them to stand up. Unless your particular perversion is very strange and you get your jollies just by making people stand up, you will be interested in more than this. And indeed, in most cases, you will get from your submissive much more control than this as part of the same *transaction*.

A seasoned submissive will typically give up a very large amount of control in response to the initial control-taking by a dominant. Indeed the control-taking action will be mostly symbolic in their case, taking large swathes of emotional, sexual and physical control over the submissive all at the one time.

Exactly what's included in this extra control will vary from submissive to submissive. It will depend on many factors, including their own conditioning and experience, their trust in you, how strongly they feel their need for control, etc.

An important thing to note is that this control is given to you as part of the initial transaction, but it still needs you to complete the process by actually recognising and asserting this control. For example, after directing your submissive to stand, you might then further tell them how you want them to stand, or tell them how you want them to address you. These subsequent acts build on or consolidate the initial transfer, and further define for both you and the submissive how, and over what, you want to assert control.

The idea of this period after the initial transfer serving to "bed down" the control transfer is very important. As well as being used by both you and your submissive as a time to get used to the idea of having taken or having given up control, respectively, it is also used by your submissive to learn and adjust to how they will be controlled—i.e. to your particular quirks—and by you to learn how your submissive reacts to being controlled. Note that this can be a time of stress or uncertainty.

Also note that we may not be talking here about conscious awareness of, or a conscious transfer, of control. All four steps of the transfer of control, and the consolidation, could be occurring subconsciously in you, in your submissive, or in you both.

For you, the dominant, consolidating and bedding down the control mainly consists of using the control, exploring the boundaries, recognising reactions and dealing with them. The main thing then, is to use the control in as wide a variety of ways as possible, and to watch what happens as a result. You and your submissive will use this to learn:

1. When and how you typically use the control,

2. How you react to it,

3. How your submissive reacts to it,

4. Any unexpected negative aspects to its use,

5. Any unexpected positive aspects to its use,

6. How well its use by you satisfies your submissive's needs,

7. And how well its use satisfies your own needs.

Both of you will be using this time of familiarisation to adapt to the new balance of control. Regularly debriefing your submissive during this can be a good way to get closer to how they are reacting and feeling.

Expanding control

Taking control by grabbing your submissive by the scruff of their neck and manhandling them to the floor doesn't mean that you have acquired control over their entire life. Taking control in such a primal manner might give you control over them physically or sexually, but it's much less likely that they'll then respond to your orders regarding their finances, their work, their family or their free time.

Once you have taken initial control then, how do you go about expanding this control into other areas of their life and being?

Well, once you have explored the control that they gave you as part of the initial transfer, and you've found its boundaries and you want more, then you will have to take more control. In other words you will have to go through another transfer-of-control process.

Consider the case where you are at a play party and you want to do something particularly perverted to an attractive submissive you meet there. You might say, "Come with me to the Comfy Chair[4]", where you proceed to do horrid and unspeakable things to them. Afterwards, however, when you are unwinding from this

---

[4]A reference to an obscure piece of torture equipment used by the infamous, mid-to-late twentieth century intellectual group known as Monty Python.

job well done, you might want this submissive to go and get you a drink. The context is different however, and the control that you took initially, and which they gave up, and which allowed you to torture them, may not include having them serve you drinks. It's possible then, that you would have to separately take more control so that they will serve you.

However, your submissive is more likely to give up control to you when the new control is similar to control you already have. If you have just manhandled them to the floor, then they're likely to also respond to orders to stand, sit, kneel and other physical acts. On the other hand if you have just manhandled them to the floor, and then tell them to write an essay on Marcel Proust you might find yourself much less lucky.

Let's look at a possible progression of control-taking:

1. Manhandle the submissive to the floor,

2. Tell them to kneel, sit, stand, present, etc.,

3. Tell them to serve food and/or drinks and correct how they do so,

4. Tell them how to undress and perform sexually,

5. Tell them how to dress in the future,

6. Give them wide guidelines for their social life, and where and with whom they can go out,

7. Tell them to discuss their major decisions of each day with you,

8. Tell them not to make major decisions—unless they need to be made immediately—without discussing them with you first,

9. Give them guidelines for making decisions,

10. Tell them that you will be making certain decisions,

11. Tell them that all decision-making authority rests with you.

Each step in the above series builds on the previous step. Bedding down, or consolidating, each step is important; in other words you don't rush through the list in a matter of just minutes, instead you stop after each step, making sure both you and your submissive are settled, before moving on to the next step. This series doesn't cover all areas of control, of course, but it is a useful example to see how you can go from one area to another.

Conclusion

I have included both consolidation of control and expansion of control in this one section because I see them both as being part of the process of creating or exploring the boundaries of the control you have over your submissive. In some cases, too, it can be hard to tell if something is in fact consolidation rather than actually expansion.

The important thing that I'd like to get across in this section, is that there is an initial contact between a dominant and a submissive where the dominant begins to take control. This can be a matter of just an instant of time. This is followed by a much longer bedding down, and defining of the extent of the control.

Things to think about

1. A dominant can explore the boundaries of their control over a submissive by giving orders or directions, and then observing any external signs of resistance or rejection by the submissive. This is fairly simple, but it leaves the submissive in a reactive role.

   Given that a control-sensitive submissive probably

has a strong interest in being controlled, how can they actively be involved in the consolidation process? How can they make their own original contributions?

2. It's easy to think about all this in terms of conscious, or aware, control. How does consolidation enter into the picture when we talk about subconscious or unconscious transfers of control?

3. Think about your own, personal "standard moves" when you first approach a submissive. What control do you directly take, and what other control do submissives generally give up to you at the same time? When you have done a "standard move" what control do you expect to have?

4. Can you list some ways in which you can leverage control you already have to acquire more control over your submissive?

2.3 Losing control

Once you've taken control from your submissive, you'd presumably want it to stay in your hot little hands until you decide to give it back. If something happens so that your submissive takes back control when you haven't actually made the moves to give it back to them, then you have two fairly significant problems (apart from the obvious one of not having the control anymore).

The first problem is that it's likely that you won't know straight away that they've taken back control. Taking back control is purely a switch in mental state. There's no outward sign that it has occurred, and the main ways you find out that it has happened is when your submissive acts in a way which you're not expecting, or when you give an order and they don't respond. It can come as a rude, and sometimes embarrassing, awakening for you when you try to assert control and find that you don't have it any more. This is a bad way[5] to find out that you have lost control.

The second problem is that there's a good chance that it's a shortcoming or fault of your own that's caused this. After all, with a control-sensitive submissive, them not having control is the state which both they and you are looking for. When they take back control, it's putting them somewhere they don't want to be.

When it is a shortcoming of yours, then you lose credibility and the submissive loses trust. They might still think that you're

---

[5]*Bad* in the sense that it can mean a loss of face in the eyes of your submissive.

a swell person and all that, but they lose trust in your ability to wield control appropriately. This makes it harder or impossible for you to subsequently take back control from them.

I'll look at a few reasons why this taking back of control can happen shortly. What you do need to understand is that taking back control is an action on the part of the submissive which doesn't involve you. They do it in their own mind without you. When they take back control they regain the ability to exercise the control you took from them. They "throw the switch" back to where it was before the initial transfer of control. This might be simple, or difficult, or next to impossible depending on the submissive's motivation, training and skill. Their motivation comes from how strongly they perceive that the control involved needs to be asserted appropriately.

Why it can occur

It could be that they take back control because it's not being used the way it needs to be.

For a control-sensitive submissive to get the benefit of being controlled, the control over them actually has to be used by their dominant. They need to feel it. It's all well and good that the dominant takes control of them, but if the dominant then doesn't do anything with the submissive, or does very little, then the submissive will feel unsatisfied. For someone with a need to be controlled, this can create the potential in their mind to rebel simply because their need is not being met. This growing and unsatisfied need can manifest itself as misbehaviour, or acting up, in a normally well-intentioned submissive[6]. They might even genuinely

---

[6] As opposed to a *SAM*—Smart-Assed Masochist—who deliberately acts up or misbehaves to get punished. Some psychotherapists consider that the aberrant behaviour of their clients is a way in which they call out for the sort of attention they need to restore their lives to some sort of balance. Similarly, by acting out or misbehaving, a submissive could conceivably be calling out for a "tightening of the leash", for the feeling of more control being asserted over them.

not know why they are acting the way they are.

As we're talking about a need, there's no question that, by definition, it must be satisfied. If the need is allowed to grow and the dominant doesn't respond, or doesn't know how to respond, or responds in a way that doesn't satisfy the need, then the potential grows and eventually the submissive will act on their own. What they might do is take back control so that they can then give it to someone else who will use it as the submissive needs it used.

Another situation in which a submissive will take back control is when the control itself needs to be exercised and the dominant either doesn't do it, or else isn't there to do it. A simple example might be when the dominant has taken control of the submissive's finances and a bill comes in and needs to be paid. If the dominant doesn't do anything about it, or has gone away and hasn't left instructions about how to deal with unexpected bills, then the submissive is under pressure to take back control and pay the bill.

The same sort of reaction could occur if one of the submissive's friends or a member of their family became ill, and they needed to go and visit, but the dominant didn't act to authorise this visit, or wasn't there to do so. The common theme here is that the submissive perceives a need for the submissive themself to act, but doesn't have the control to do so, and the dominant doesn't act.

A final example situation, often one which develops over a period of time, and which can cause a submissive to take back control, is when control is misused—as far as the submissive can tell—by the dominant. If, for example, the dominant uses their control to have the submissive hurt other people, or behave illegally, or in ways that go against the submissive's own morals, then they'll feel pressure to rebel and take back control. One such case might not be enough to trigger them, but a regular pattern of such abuse might cause the pressure to build up until the submissive "cracks".

It's not only that the control is being abused that's a problem here. A regular pattern of misuse will also condition the submissive to associate their submission with negative feelings, or with hurt to other people, or with hurt to themselves. For a control-sensitive submissive, this will mean that over time:

1. They'll be less motivated to give up control, and
2. They'll likely start to suppress any need they feel, with possible long-term negative consequences.

Preventing it from occurring

I would say that there are two main things that you can use to help prevent you losing control. They are experience and structure. I will talk a little bit about structure here and then go into it in more detail in the management chapter of this book.

Experience with a range of submissives in a variety of situations, and over long periods of time, will give you a feel for the sorts of things which can create the *control stress* which can cause the submissive to try to take back control. You learn about these both by observation, and by debriefing after an incident has occurred, and by encouraging and helping the submissive to communicate when they're feeling nervous or stressed, even if they don't know why.

Experience can then help you to avoid the situations where control stress occurs. More importantly, it can help you create a structure to impose on the submissive. Expressed simply, a structure is a set of rules and priorities you impose on a submissive which exert your control over them even in your absence. You can create a structure just by saying something as simple as,

> *"If choices or decisions need to be made which I would normally make, and I am not around to make them, I expect you to do your best to try to choose as I would. In all such cases, I expect you to let me*

know the situation and your choices as soon as possible after the fact, so that I can make any necessary corrections."

By saying the above you are doing two things:

1. Imposing your control in your absence—even without being specific—by setting guidelines, and
2. You're also asserting your authority to come back and correct the submissive later.

You might consider this latter as control over the fine-tuning of the submissive.

This simple structure means that your submissive need never act on their own. Your control is always there.

It's likely that a more sophisticated or complex structure is needed for some submissives or some situations, but this basic idea can impose your control on a continuous basis.

Damaging to the submissive

Being put in a situation where they need to take back control is damaging for a submissive. Generally they'll have a lot tied up in their self-image. Even though they are forced into making the choice of the only possible action, i.e. taking back control, they'll suffer because they have taken control from their dominant, because they've possibly disobeyed, and because they have likely acted against their own self-image as a "good submissive".

More than this, the submissive might see all this as the "beginning of the end" because they'll know that after having taken back control once they can do it again, and indeed subsequent times will be, by virtue of the submissive's previous experience, easier. Being under pressure to stay obedient when the submissive has never taken back control in their entire submissive life, is a very different proposition to feeling that same pressure and knowing first-hand what to do to take back control. Knowing that taking back control is a real possibility to deal with a situation, is probably not where any submissive ever really wants to be.

Conclusion

Losing control is bad. It hurts both the submissive and the dominant. Maybe both come away from the experience older and wiser, but perhaps better planning, in the form of more comprehensive standing orders or structure, and a better understanding of the consequences and responsibility of control can lead to it happening less often.

Things to think about

1. Talk to a submissive or two and ask them about times when they've felt a need or desire to act either against their dominant's orders or wishes, or when they've felt a need to make up their own mind to act because their dominant can't or won't. What were the situations? How could the dominant have prevented the submissive experiencing these conflicts? Would different standing orders have helped? Which standing orders?

2. How can a dominant regain the confidence of a submissive when the submissive has had to take back control due to a shortcoming of the dominant?

3. Is there a way a dominant can tell they've lost control without finding out first-hand by giving an order and not having it obeyed? How many ways are there to do this?

4. When a submissive takes back control in a given situation, exactly how much do they take back? All of it? Some of it? If they don't take all control back, can the control the

dominant still has be used as a lever to help regain the lost control?

5. What have you learned, as a result of experience, about losing control which you didn't know when you first started taking control of submissives?

2.4 Reward and encouragement

Society largely dictates the contexts in which either taking control or giving control are "good things"—like a waiter taking control of where a patron sits in the restaurant, or a policeman directing the movements of passersby near a crime scene or accident, or a fireman keeping spectators clear of a burning building. We learn to do this, to give up our control easily if our role is that of passerby, or to easily take and assert control if our role is that of fireman.

For the rest of the time, society generally encourages us to be individuals and to take responsibility for ourselves, to take control of our own lives, and to run them ourselves, and to leave everyone else alone control-wise. Society presents us with images of keeping control of our home life, our friendships, our sex lives, what we wear, our recreation, our TV viewing habits and so on. Indeed, the law further encourages this by making us responsible for our own actions once we reach a certain age.

So, we learn when it's a good thing to give up control to avoid friction with society-at-large, and for the rest of the time to tenaciously keep control to ourselves. For a control-sensitive individual, be they dominant or submissive, it's necessary to overcome some of this learning.

Individual experience plays a part in this. Someone with a drive to be controlled is generally not just going to fall into a satisfying dominant/submissive relationship straight away. Often it will be the case, before they're fully aware of their need and are able to manage it or find an appropriate outlet, that their need is going to be pushing to express itself. For these people, it's easy to get into a relationship that is close—but not close enough—to what they need. In fact, society mandates that most relationships will not be close enough. What can happen for these submissives, is that things go wrong, and they get unpleasant reinforcement that they should be keeping themselves in control, rather than giving up control to someone else. Part of it is that they experience their need and they try to push it into a form which matches what society says is acceptable. This is typically not successful.

Someone who has a drive to be in control—to take and assert control—is not in a much better situation. Taking control of another person, using them, in circumstances not fitting society's patterns, is generally frowned upon, and people with that drive are often forced, as are submissives, to suppress it and find something more acceptable to do with their energy.

Rewarding control transfer

For control-sensitive individuals, a transfer of control is a reward in itself. Each time it occurs it will reinforce the natural tendencies of the dominant or submissive concerned, and it will tend to undo or overcome the conditioning against expressing their need which they'd received in the past. Of course, satisfying any need can be a deeply rewarding experience—ditto for satisfying the need to be controlled or to be in control.

Is this reward enough? The "itch" gets scratched, the need gets met, and the hunger gets satisfied… doesn't it? Can it be better?

If the role of the dominant is to take control, to consolidate and expand control, then part of that is also using strategies to help the submissive give up as much control as possible. Using triggers, such as pulling the submissive's head back by the hair, have an immediate effect. But these are existing triggers or existing conditioning. In the longer term, actively rewarding the submissive each time they give up control will also serve to overcome any previous negative conditioning. I'd argue that rewarding and encouraging the giving up of control, particularly in the early days of a relationship, or with a submissive with limited experience, is a must in order to let their needs fully appear.

What sort of rewards or encouragements can you use?

When you are exploring your submissive, poking around the boundaries of the control which they've given up, you'll likely come across resistance or fear. Trying to push or force them to give up control, or to expose themselves, isn't always the answer. Behaving so they feel that they can safely give up control to you without being hurt, or so that they can expose themselves to you safely, can create such a potential so instead of having to be pulled through their resistance and out into the open, that they'll rush forward themselves, relieved to finally be able to let themselves out. This is encouragement by simple acceptance.

Recognising your submissive's progress in some way, noticing the efforts they make to talk to you about their inner feelings, or noticing the the work they do to overcome their fears and expose intimate control to you, is also important. Just accepting and using what they give is part of it, but also recognising the work they have put in, and making them aware of your pleasure is often a boost for them. Just stroking their hair and telling them they've done well, or thanking them for their effort for you, can be enough.

Conclusion

If society tends to suppress or discourage some forms of control-taking or control-giving, then creating a micro-society of your own—even if just in your own house, a micro-society where the people in it accept, or even actively encourage, taking and giving control, accept explorations of control, and also provide opportunities to share with others of similar bent, then any natural drives in these directions will tend to surface again. Finding like-minded people, maybe in niches of the world of BDSM, can be a major and positive step forward.

On an individual level, you can recognise and encourage the steps your submissive makes to give up more control to you. Talk to them, and find the fears and conditioning that they've had in the past, and help them find ways to overcome them.

Things to think about

1. What sort of society would be ideal to allow a dominant to actually express all aspects of his drive to be in control?

2. What sort of society would be ideal to allow a submissive to fully express themselves? What aspects of our current society get in the way of this? What is there in your life now which gets in the way?

3. How can you create a micro-society in which more, or all, of a dominant's or submissive's needs can be expressed and satisfied?

4. The law generally says that an individual is responsible for their own actions. Is this something that can limit a transfer of control? What about the responsibility that comes with being in control? To what extent do you need to take care that the person you control doesn't get into trouble with the law through following your instructions? What do you do if they do get into trouble? Will the law recognise in any way that responsibility was transferred from your submissive to you? If so, in what circumstances?

2.5 Giving back control

Just as taking control is a process with a clearly defined series of steps, so too is giving back control. Indeed, it is actually much the same process, and as such it involves actions by both the dominant and the submissive. Many people pay a lot of attention to the initial taking of control, and concentrate on getting that right, without paying the same attention to what happens when they give back control. This can and does lead to it being done poorly or incompletely, and to confusion and disorientation in the submissive.

Communication is always important at any time, but in the context of giving back control it means that the intention of both the dominant's actions and the submissive's actions are clear to each other so that each can respond appropriately. The best response is that in each's mind the "switch" which was thrown, when control was first taken by the dominant, is thrown back to its original position, i.e. the submissive is back in control and dominant is not.

Here are two actions which the dominant might make to give back control:

1. Remove the submissive's collar,

2. Say, "I release you".

These are both very simple, but would normally be near the end of a longer ritual wherein both the submissive's and the dominant's expectations are built up in advance of the release. Indeed, just doing either of the above actions *in vuoto*—with no build up—would probably leave both participants feeling as if something were missing. Expectation and build-up increase the symbolism and the impact of the act, increasing at the some time the force with which the "switch" is thrown back.

Once the dominant gives control back, it's the turn of the submissive to take it up. The final step of the initial transfer of control, when the dominant first took control of the submissive, was to assert the control. When the submissive takes back control, they also need to do the same thing—they need to assert the control. What they actually do will depend on what control was taken in the first place. Here are some examples:

1. If the submissive had been expected to kneel most of the time, then once they were released they could rise from the kneeling position,

2. They could begin referring to the dominant by name rather than, "Sir", or, "Master",

3. They could get their own coffee without asking permission,

4. They could make their own mind up about what they wear.

What all these things have in common is that the submissive is asserting and deciding for themselves. There will be a symbolic component in this. Over the course of a long relationship, the dominant may have taken and asserted control over a wide range of aspects of the submissive. One or two simple actions can't demonstrate that the submissive has taken back control over every single aspect of themselves, but can be symbolic and represent every single aspect.

Giving back control after a long-term transfer

Decision-making is a learned and practiced skill. If a submissive had been under the control of a dominant for a long period, then they may need time to relearn the skills and/or knowledge required to competently make their own decisions again. This isn't directly an issue of being or not being under control, but is a consequence of having been under control. As such, I would argue that it's part of the responsibility that the dominant acquired when they first took control of the submissive, to help the submissive regain these skills. I explore this more in the chapter on Management.

Consolidation

Just as there is a phase of consolidation of control when the dominant first takes control, there is also a phase of consolidation when the submissive takes back control. This goes beyond what the submissive does when they initially have control given back to them. The initial acts made by the submissive when they first get back control are, as I previously said, likely to be at least partially symbolic. The consolidation that follows makes this control concrete. It involves exploring and asserting control over all areas where the dominant has been. You might like to consider it as being that the submissive doesn't fully have control back until they have asserted their own control over all areas where the dominant previously has been.

This can be an active process with the submissive deliberately and systematically consolidating their control over themselves. In some cases, the dominant can help get this start by putting the submissive in situations where they have to make choices and decisions for themselves. Here are some examples of things the dominant can do, after releasing a submissive, to help begin the consolidation:

1. Refer to the submissive by name instead of "girl" or "boy",

2. Ask the (ex-)submissive what they want for dinner,

3. Ask permission to use the bathroom while in the submissive's house,

4. Not suggest options but make the submissive come up with them,

5. Stop using their usual dominant tone of voice,

6. Stop being imperative.

What can go wrong

A difference between taking control and giving back control is that the dominant is usually around after the initial taking of control to consolidate and reinforce the transfer. On the other hand, it's common for the dominant not to be there soon after control is given back. This can mean that when control is given back there might be no one to help the submissive to consolidate the taking-back of control.

In such a situation, an inexperienced submissive could find themselves in difficulty—possibly aided and abetted by overwhelming emotions. Reactions to submissive experiences can come hours or days after the actual experience has ended, and it's probably appropriate in most instances to ensure that the submissive has access to some form of aftercare from the dominant concerned, or access to some other means of getting help or support.

The dominant isn't off the hook immediately after they've given control back to the submissive. The consolidation phase which the submissive has to go through is something which the dominant may be able to help with, particularly if there is any confusion regarding how much control has been given back to the submissive. Poor phrasing when giving back control can lead to this sort of confusion. For example, after meeting a submissive and playing one evening, a dominant might say, "I release you;

I've finished with you for tonight", which leaves the submissive confused about whether the dominant has released them completely or just for the evening. Resolving this confusion might involve just clarifying what has been said, or it might even need a further, and formal, giving back of control.

Another problem is that the submissive might refuse to take back control when it's given to them. This can be an obvious and blunt refusal, or a less obvious inability to take control and responsibility, possibly accompanied by confusion. If this happens, you need to discuss it with the submissive, and work out what's stopping them taking back control. All the various possibilities of why, and what to do about them are, unfortunately, beyond the scope of this book.

Conclusion

Although it's at the tail end of a dominant/submissive experience, giving back control merits as much attention as any of the other activities in which either the dominant or the submissive are involved. The responsibility of both the dominant and the submissive to ensure proper closure means that this should be a time of great focus. It is the last opportunity when many loose ends can be tidied. Rather than just an afterthought, this time of closure is what gives the total experience it's final colour.

Things to think about

1. What other situations or questions can you give to a submissive, once you've released them, to help them consolidate their own control over themselves?

2. Is it appropriate for the dominant to stay around once control has been given back? Can the subsequent presence or actions of the dominant interfere with the submissive's consolidation of control over themselves? Is it harder for the

submissive to focus on themselves when the dominant is still around?

3. What else can the dominant do to help the submissive consolidate the return of control?

4. What other actions might a dominant make to indicate that they are giving control back to the submissive?

5. What other actions might a submissive perform to indicate that they have taken back control?

6. What sort of ritual do you use to give back control to a submissive?

7. Instead of just saying, "I release you", what's a better and more comprehensive formula?

2.6 Focus of control

Once a submissive has given up control, how do they know who to obey? I use the word "know" to mean having an awareness or understanding at any of the conscious, subconscious or unconscious levels.

If the submissive has given up control, why don't they just obey everyone?

The answer is that part of the control transfer process is *focus*. And initially, at least, the dominant who takes control has this focus.

Recognising that focus is a separate component of the transfer process is important because, as we'll see shortly, once control has been taken from the submissive, the focus may be transferred between dominants.

Put in other words, control only needs to be taken from a submissive once, and may then be passed from one dominant to another. And, generally speaking, changing who has the control—or focus—over a submissive, is far easier than taking control in the first place.

Let us look at the thoughts of a submissive called "Y" and a dominant called "X":

Two thoughts	
Submissive Y	**Dominant X**
"I am under the control of X"	"I am in control of Y"

Contrast these with the thoughts of another submissive (called "A") and another dominant (called "B"):

Another two thoughts	
Submissive A	**Dominant B**
"I am under control"	"I am in control"

The difference between these two examples is that of knowing where this focus of control lies. In the first example, both the dominant and the submissive are fully aware of who they control, or are controlled by, respectively. In the second example, this awareness isn't there.

Where does this focus, or awareness of direction, come from?

In an initial taking of control—as outlined in the earlier section on the process (section 2.1 on page 49)—it's usually obvious because both the submissive and the dominant are directly involved. However when control is passed from one dominant to another, there's a chance that this focus can become lost or muddled leaving either the submissive, or one, or both of the dominants, confused.

When another dominant needs to be in control of a particular submissive, the alternative to having a transfer of focus between the dominants is that the submissive takes back the control completely, and then gives it up again to the second dominant as part of a second control transfer. For a control-sensitive submissive, this is clearly less than ideal because their need is to be controlled, not to be in control, even if the state of "being in control" only lasts as long as it takes for the second dominant to take control. It is also not ideal for the dominants because of the extra work required.

However, in a large group of dominants and submissives—where there are enough dominants around so that the submissive sees them all as one large homogenous authority—a sort of *continuity of dominance* is assured. Control releasing and subsequent re-taking by a second dominant is not required here. The submissive will usually be focussed on one particular dominant, but can transfer her focus to another dominant in that same group fairly easily.

Reaction against the transfer of focus

Although the transfer of focus is lighter and easier than an initial transfer of control, it can still fail. The worst thing that can happen is that the submissive reacts against the transfer and tries to take back control. Here are two examples of what might make a submissive react this way:

1. The control initially was and is only on offer to a particular individual, e.g. that submissive's lover/dominant, who tries to give it to someone else,

2. The dominant who is taking over is someone the submissive doesn't trust at some level.

It's not instantaneous

Transfer of focus doesn't always happen instantaneously. It might take some time for the transfer to become bedded down in the mind of the submissive and the dominants. During this time the submissive might continue to be responsive to the dominant who gave up control over them, as well as to the dominant who took it up. This bedding down process will go faster when the dominant taking up control actively asserts that control over the submissive as soon as possible, and as often as necessary until it is settled.

The more the submissive is used to transferring focus, the faster it will go, too.

Act of transfer

As with a complete transfer of control, there is an *act of transfer* where focus is concerned. It might be simply be the dominant saying to the submissive, "I am now giving you completely to Z", and then to Z, "Here. Take this submissive!" This might also be accompanied with some form of written or verbal contract. Alternatively, the act of transfer of focus might be something more symbolic, such as the dominant handing the submissive's leash—to which the submissive is still attached—to Z, or it could be something more physical, such as the dominant actually grabbing the submissive by the arm or hair and passing them to Z. Because there is no direct way of adjusting the submissive's brain to this new situation, clear and very unambiguous communication is a must for this work. Without clear communication, Z might think, for example, he is in control when the submissive doesn't.

The two dominants

It's interesting that this transfer from one dominant to another has many of the same characteristics as an initial transfer of control from a submissive to a dominant, notably:

1. Control must be available or offered (by the first dominant),
2. Control must be taken or accepted (by the second dominant),
3. Control must be given up (by the first dominant),
4. Control must be asserted (by the second dominant).

Along with these same steps, many of the same mental changes occur in the two dominants as well. That is, the "switch" gets thrown to "I am no longer in control", or to the "I am now in control" position, respectively.

Differences

Some of the differences between a submissive-to-dominant transfer of control and a dominant-to-dominant transfer are:

1. In the first case, two people are involved. In the second, there are three, with a corresponding increase in possibilities for communication breakdowns,

2. As well as the act that closes the transfer from the first dominant, the dominant receiving the control should also act to trigger the transfer of focus in the submissive from the first dominant to themselves. That is to say, that the first dominant must clearly relinquish control in a way that is unambiguous to both the second dominant AND the submissive, and then the second dominant must clearly take and assert control over the submissive. This latter must be apparent both to the submissive and to the first dominant.

Conclusion

Many people have an intuitive grasp of the basic ideas and problems behind simply taking control of a submissive. Passing a submissive from one dominant to another opens up a recognisably similar, but not same, can of worms. The two most important differences are:

1. A transfer of focus is usually less demanding than the initial taking of control,

2. The transfer of focus now includes three people, instead of two, with a corresponding increase in communication problems.

Things to think about

1. I listed a couple of things that could cause a submissive to react against a transfer of focus. What are some others?

2. What are some other acts which can be used to transfer a submissive's focus of control to another dominant?

3. I said that the worst thing which can happen when a dominant attempts to transfer a submissive's focus is that the

submissive attempts to take back control? How else might they react?

2.7 Safewords

Many practitioners of BDSM use *safewords*. These are signal words or actions which have been agreed on between players before a scene begins. When the person being done to, i.e. the submissive or bottom, says one of these agreed words, or does one of these agreed actions, it is a signal to the other person. Typically it's an indication that there's a problem and that things need to either slow down or stop. Common safewords are words like "red" (meaning: I'm in serious trouble), "yellow" (I am having some difficulty. Slow down!), or "green" (No problems. Go faster!). When someone is gagged or would otherwise have difficulty speaking, a squeaky toy can be used to create a signal. Some submissives like to hold on to something, like a ball, and when they drop it, this is their "red" signal.

Safewords are often an excellent idea. When two people first get together, safewords can give confidence to both of them, and can also establish a feedback system which helps them play safely. Safewords have strong implications for control though. The main issue comes not when they are used, but when they are agreed upon.

An agreement between a submissive and a dominant is a form of contract. Suppose the agreement is that when the submissive says the word "red", that the dominant will immediately cease inflicting whatever they are inflicting on the submissive. This agreement takes control away from the dominant and gives it to the submissive. It gives the submissive a button they can push which is guaranteed to make the dominant do what the submissive wants, i.e. stop, start or go faster. In a control-sensitive relationship, this may not be a positive step forward.

In spite of hearing the "red" safeword from the submissive, a dominant might be 100% certain that going further will be OK. If they do proceed though, there are serious risks for both the dominant and the relationship. Firstly, the submissive can then rightly and loudly proclaim that the dominant is not to be trusted, and that the submissive was abused because the dominant had continued the scene when the submissive had clearly signalled for it to stop.

The dominant also loses the submissive's trust and, possibly, the submissive's future company.

I am not arguing against safewords here because, at their core, safewords establish a new channel of communication between the submissive and the dominant, one that is particularly useful for submissives who become either completely or partially non-verbal during scenes. As the current theme is control, what I do want to argue for here, is a way of using safewords so that the control dynamic retains intact, i.e. the dominant stays in control.

Maintaining feedback similar to that gained by safewords, but without the negative control or trust consequences that I just mentioned a couple of paragraphs ago, can be achieved by using safewords in an *advisory only* role, and without any agreement as to how the dominant will react when he hears them. In this new scheme, it'd probably be best not to call them "safewords" any more, because people hearing the term would automatically assume—possibly in spite of your best explanations—that you mean the words which guarantee the dominant will stop what they're doing, when that's not what you mean at all.

Let's call them instead, *advisory-words*. Here's an example of how you might use them:

> *You are about to do a scene with your submissive. You say to them, "In this scene, we're not going to use safewords. We're going to use advisory-words*

instead, because I just want to be able to get simple feedback from you about where you're at. When you say the word, "red", I'll know that you are having difficulty and I'll take that into account when deciding what to do next. When you say, "green", I'll know that you're feeling really comfortable with what's happening. When you say, "orange", I'll take that as a signal that you're starting to feel edgy."

In this example, you can see it's clear, regardless of whether your submissive uses an advisory-word or not, that you stay in control and that you decide what happens. Your submissive uses these advisory-words simply to give you information without having any expectation about what you'll do with it.

You can probably also see that using advisory-words is a step forward in the area of trust. Your submissive does have to give up an important control to you—that of being able to regulate the scene themselves, trusting that you will deal with them positively and that they'll not get harmed.

By using advisory-words a dominant also explicitly takes on extra responsibility. With safewords the submissive is able to regulate the scene to some extent, and retains and shares accountability when things go wrong. With advisory-words, this is no longer the case. The submissive loses the ability to regulate the scene, and the dominant has to pick up that extra burden plus the concomitant responsibility.

An aspect of this added responsibility is that the submissive needs to accept that the dominant, being human, is going to make mistakes from time to time. They have to develop the trust that allows them to continue through the times when mistakes are made, knowing that their dominant is skilled, is doing their best, but that things go wrong anyway. Indeed, even if the submissive were to remain in control via safewords, there's no guarantee that errors and mistakes wouldn't be made anyway!

Return to safewords

Advisory-words aren't for everyone, of course. If you've just met someone at a party, and you want to play a little bit, then using safewords gives both of you comfort and safety, and also limits how much control the submissive gives up. Maybe later, sometime in the future, once you know each other better, you can move on to advisory-words.

Safewords and advisory-words aren't infallible though. Using a safeword can indicate that there is a problem, but the absence of a safeword does not indicate that there is no problem. An unconscious submissive, for example, cannot say "red", even though there's clearly a problem. A submissive who is happily in some state of euphoria or sub-space, is also not necessarily capable of judging when they are being seriously damaged and may not indicate "red" when they should.

Safewords can also be missed. In a party environment, for example, with loud music or lots of background noise, the dominant may not hear a safeword. Or they might be looking somewhere else when the submissive drops the signal ball, and not notice that it's gone when they look back.

Ultimately, a dominant relying on hearing a safeword to know when to stop is relying on an unreliable source. Safewords and advisory-words are just an extra bit of information, along with many others which you should be using. Other forms of feedback, such as watching how your submissive is reacting, by talking to them from time to time, touching them, looking at their eyes, and so forth, all give you more information with which to better control the scene.

Pre-verbal

It's often a characteristic of the submissive experience, that the submissive has trouble speaking, or can't speak at all. I talk about this speaking difficulty in more detail elsewhere in this book, but a point to make here is that the use of an agreed signal, or of a couple of agreed words, for a submissive in such a *pre-verbal* state, can allow them to communicate what's important without having to go through the complex mental processes involved in turning ideas into sentences. No explanation is required, because the limited vocabulary of pre-agreed phrases or signals says what needs to be said without disturbing the submissive's state of mind [much].

Conclusion

Control isn't always taken and given in the way I've talked about in previous sections of this book. Control can also be given up by agreement. This is a form of contract entered into by two people, in which one agrees to do X when the other does Y. Safewords are an example of this. This sort of agreement is also a lot more common than you might expect.

Advisory-words are a technique which still allows the submissive to communicate, but without having the dominant give up control.

Both safewords and advisory-words have strong implications for control. Not necessarily for taking or giving up control, but for staying in control of a situation.

Things to think about

1. What agreements have you entered into with your submissive—possibly as concessions for some reason—which give them control or, at least, allow them to retain control?

2. When have safewords not worked for you?

3. Are there any situations where having safewords or

advisory-words would have negative or harmful consequences?

4. Some people say that with trust and familiarity, a dominant and a submissive find safewords and advisory-words to be unnecessary. Is this so? Sometimes so? Always so?

2.8 Control-taking and privacy

As I mentioned earlier, taking control requires an act by the dominant. The dominant actually has to do or say something to take control. Dominants do all sorts of things all day, but not all of them are control-taking acts in the sense that I've been using so far in this book. In this section, I want to consider what is, and what isn't, an act of control-taking, and how this relates to personal privacy.

Suppose you meet someone on the street, and you shake their hand. Have you performed "the act"? Maybe you were the aggressor who reached out, took their hand and vigorously shook it. Certainly you took physical control of their hand for that brief instant of time, but was it an act of control-taking in any dominant/submissive sense?

Or, let's look at it another way: you have a new submissive partner in your lustful possession, and you want to do something to assert control over them. Would you consider vigorously shaking their hand as a way of doing this? Why not? What would you consider? What acts are likely to trigger a transfer of control in them, and what acts are unlikely to trigger a transfer?

It's clear that not all acts have the same impact in the control arena. Here's a short table of acts, some of which probably do trigger a submissive response, and some of which probably don't trigger such a response. Hopefully you can see something in common in each column.

Acts which can trigger a submissive response	Acts which don't trigger a submissive response
Stepping up close and towering over a submissive	Shaking hands
Grabbing the hair on the back of a submissive's head and pulling their head back	Hugging
Instructing the submissive to kneel	Gesturing the submissive to go through a doorway before you
Wrapping your fingers gently around the submissive's neck	Telling the submissive to answer the telephone
Grabbing the submissive and throwing them bodily to the floor	

The thing I had in mind when I wrote the above table was *privacy*. Many acts which actually do take control of a person in some way, are so common, at least in our society, that they no longer have any real impact. They are accepted as part of the normal behaviour which lubricates our society, and are seen as perfectly ordinary in normal inter-personal relationships. All the acts in the second column of the table fall into this category—they aren't private in any way.

Even many behaviours which once would have been called personal or private, have lost the lustre of being truly personal. Being naked or topless in front of some stranger, doesn't have the same quality of invasiveness that it had, say, 50 or even 20 years ago. Being naked or topless in public, in some contexts, is now even widely accepted—such as on nude beaches or in Mardi Gras parades. Sexual intercourse too, is far less private now than in the past. Indeed, many women regard sexual intercourse as a likely and even desirable consequence of first dates.

As a general principle, I'm going to say that to assert control over a submissive requires some way of asserting control that is private, invasive and personal. Importantly, it must be perceived as all these things by the submissive themselves.

When considering what to assert control over, you should consider:

- Private parts of the body. It's important to note here, that we're not talking only about those parts of the body that are generally considered as "private parts". We're actually talking about those parts which the submissive feels are private and personal to them. Surprisingly, their breasts and genitals may not be as personal to them as their neck or face, for example,

- Private behaviour. The submissive may not find that being watched as they're getting dressed is very personal. Or being watched as they're sitting on the toilet. Sexual intercourse itself might not even be private, but the choice of where or with whom they perform this is usually very private,

- Private thoughts and fantasies,

- Personal things done to them. Shaking the submissive's hand is very likely not personal, but grabbing their neck, pulling their head back, handling them roughly or stripping the clothes off them, could all be very invasive and personal to them.

Conclusion

Like always, when you are working with a submissive you are—or should be—trying to trigger, manipulate and control their feelings and reactions. Your armoury includes your understanding of them and your empathy for what they're feeling. While textbook acts and phrases might work some of the time, your understanding of their own perception of their privacy, and of what is personal to them gives you a very fertile work area when you are exploring control over them. In other words, work on the acts, the parts of their body, the ideas and thoughts that they genuinely and deeply feel belong solely and exclusively to them.

Things to think about

1. In the first section of this chapter, I used someone coming into your office and telling you to stand up and follow them, as an example of taking control. Is there an element of privacy in this example?

2. Are privacy and invasiveness the only criteria which determine the impact or effectiveness of a control-taking act from the point of view of a submissive?

Chapter 3

Communication

I'd like to now turn my attention to communication.

In its simplest form, communication is about getting an idea from one person's head into the head of another person, usually by means of words—written or spoken—or by gestures or actions.

You might be inclined to think that it's enough to say what you mean as clearly and succinctly as possible, but this belies the complexity and sophistication of the way humans communicate with each other. Going beyond speech there are at least actions, gestures, tone of voice, postures, smells—such as musk—and facial expressions. At any particular time most, but not all, of these are under conscious control. This often means that along with what you think you're saying, your subconscious mind and your unconscious are also sending out messages, either modulating your voice with hidden-to-you meaning, or else adapting your posture and movements to reflect what they are trying to express.

There are some unusual characteristics to communication in a relationship based on dominance and submission. In most other relationships, the responsibility for good communication between the participants is shared out according to ability and skill—for example, adults talking to children generally have a greater responsibility to ensure that the right messages are being sent and received, simply because adults generally have more experience and wider understanding.

In control-sensitive relationships however, it's not just ability and skill at communication which are important—control enters the picture, too. In an ideal world, the highly-skilled dominant would take control of communication with the submissive, regulating ways of communicating, ways of speaking, resolving difficulties when ideas aren't getting across clearly, etc. This isn't always the case. A less-skilled dominant might well find themselves at a disadvantage with a submissive who is more talented at communication, such as one who is a teacher, public speaker or writer.

It would be easy, in such a situation, for the dominant to lose, or give up, control over communication to the submissive. But here the dominant needs to be aware of the control involved, and the value of better communication must be weighed against the control acquired by the submissive.

Another interesting characteristic is that, even with the same partner, you aren't always talking to the same person. What I mean is that if, for example, your partner is a submissive then you, as their dominant, will have to talk differently to them depending on their state of mind (headspace). How you talk to them when they're in deep sub-space, for example, is going to be very different to how you talk to them when you're both shopping in the supermarket.

In the rest of this chapter I am going to be exploring these and other aspects of communication particularly, of course, as it enters into dominance & submission.

3.1 Division of labour

In a world where all things are equal—including the talents, skills and rank of each individual—we'd all take equal responsibility for making communication work, for making sure that we say what we mean in a way which is likely to be correctly interpreted, and that we listen and interpret in such a way as to get the correct and original sense of the communication. In reality, it is rarely the case that we are equally skilled and responsible.

If you consider an adult talking to a child, then you might realise that a child is simply not capable of understanding concepts and ideas as sophisticated as those which an adult might have. At the same time, a child's limited experience with the world makes it likely that they can't put themselves in the shoes of the adult and second guess what the adult means by something. This places the majority of the responsibility for getting the message across properly on the adult's shoulders.

The listener involved in any communication generally interprets what is said on the basis of their experience. You might say "tree" while thinking of a tall, majestic oak tree, but the person listening to you is thinking of a decorated Christmas tree. Both, of course, are trees, but the images and feelings associated with each are very different. It comes down to the fact that the listener effectively has choices about how they interpret what you say. There is no rule that says that they have to interpret what you say the way you meant it. Choice equals control, and as we're talking about control-sensitive people and relationships, it's definitely worth our while here to consider choice in communication.

Here's an example from the world of dominance and submission. Imagine that you tell your submissive to "allow their hair to grow long at the back". Maybe you like long hair for the look, or maybe you also like long hair because it gives you something to hold on to. As it stands, such an order leaves your submissive with quite a lot of flexibility about what they do with the hair. They can just let it grow, they can wear it plaited, they can trim it regularly to make sure it's all the same length, or they can have it permed or coloured.

By telling them simply to, "allow their hair to grow long at the back", you've given them an order, but at the same time you've also given them freedom. They won't, as a result of this order, be able to feel tightly or strictly controlled. The reason they can't feel tightly controlled is because they have a very wide choice in how they interpret what you meant.

For a dominant and a submissive, the responsibility for ensuring that communication works properly in both directions must lie with the dominant. It is the dominant who must be in control of communication, just as it is the dominant who needs to be in control of other aspects of the submissive's life and relationship with them.

So, how does a dominant control communication? Here are some ideas to consider:

1. You can't directly control what goes on in your submissive's mind when you say something, but you can learn about their past experiences, and you can take note of their previous reactions to what you say in different circumstances so that you can closely predict their reactions. For example, are they unusually sensitive to criticism, insecure about some aspect of themselves, shy, or stubborn regarding new ideas?

2. Your submissive will interpret what you say or do in con-

junction with other cues which you give out. For example, your posture and the look on your face will combine with the tone of your voice, and with the actual words you say to give the complete picture. This is one reason why written-only communication, such as e-mail, is prone to being misinterpreted more easily than face-to-face communication. To make sure that your submissive gets the right idea from you, make an effort to consciously add as many cues as you can to help get the right message across. These cues can be things such as gestures, postures or facial expressions that reinforce, or add depth, to what you are saying. A couple of examples might be: using hand gestures towards the floor at the same time as you tell them to kneel, or wearing a stern facial expression at the same time as you are admonishing them.

3. Your submissive will be predisposed to interpreting what you say and do in different ways according to their expectations. These expectations are often related to where they are—both geographically, such as indoors, outdoors, or in which room of the house—and where they are mentally and spiritually, and are related to what's going on around them at the time. For example, holding the cane you normally use to discipline them while talking about housework, will give them an entirely different slant on what you are saying than if you were holding just a cup of coffee,

4. Have them explain back to you what they think you mean by something. This is asserting control by having them do something—i.e. explain—and by requiring that they do understand the way you want. It also gives you valuable and direct feedback as you see how they initially interpreted what you said.

Conclusion

Communication requires real effort from both sides. This section has looked briefly at strategies which you can use to put yourself in the driver's seat and keep yourself there. The goal is control, and communication especially is one of the areas which is available for your consideration and attention.

Things to think about

1. Suppose you strike your naked submissive's rear end with a riding crop three times. How do they know why? How do they know what this action is supposed to mean? Is it punishment? Is it motivation? How can you guarantee that there is no confusion?

2. How do you make sure that you have understood something which your submissive has explained to you? Do you get them to explain it a second time in a different way? Do you tell them what you understood and have them correct you? What ramifications can this process have as far as your control over them is concerned?

3.2 Submissive logic

An important characteristic of communication with a submissive is the way they mentally process what happens to them. How they interpret what is said or done to them is going to vary according to the headspace that they're in. One of these headspaces is, of course, sub-space... but it isn't the only one.

Let's first consider the relationship between the dominant and submissive themselves. From the submissive's point of view, this includes the experience of being dominated or controlled by the dominant as part of communication itself. Amongst other things, this is contained in the attitude that the dominant expresses towards the submissive, and for a control-sensitive submissive this experience alone is of significant value. Another way of saying this, is that the submissive can have the rewarding feeling of being controlled simply as a reaction to what the dominant is saying to them and how they say it. Because this feeling can be very valuable and satisfying, the submissive is naturally going to resist anything that might interfere with it. This can and does include starting to say something themselves. If they were to speak, it could break the flow which they are experiencing, and so they might be inclined not to speak.

It's important for a dominant to be aware of this. They might have given the submissive instructions to query the dominant about something they don't understand, or to tell the dominant when something is bothering or distracting them (e.g. a cramp), but because the submissive is deep in the experience of what's coming from the dominant, they hesitate to say anything.

You might call this a type of sub-space, but it can be one where the submissive isn't actually non-verbal—as can occur in some forms of sub-space—it's just that they don't want to speak. They are avoiding it.

Another aspect of this, is that submissives sometimes see anything critical which they say to their dominant as being attempts to take control. To overcome this, the dominant can make it clear that what the submissive says is taken as being *information only*, and that the dominant takes this into consideration, along with everything else that's happening, when making decisions.

Sub-space often has characteristics of simplicity. I don't mean that a submissive in sub-space is less intelligent than when they're in "adult" mode, just that they've basically shed the complexities of being a modern human being. Their minds tend to function in a elementary manner. Problem-solving skills and the ability to speak can easily disappear. In some ways, you end up talking to them and dealing with them as if they were a child (e.g. "Good girl!"). They aren't a child, of course, because many of the things which make them an adult remain—such as their knowledge, previous experience, and their reactions learned through previous experience—but what you say and do has to be simple and obvious, or else they're likely not to get it or to misunderstand. Simply put, concepts and ideas which they could handle with ease when not in "space", become gobbledygook when they are in "space".

They can't understand teasing or taunting

Handling teasing and taunting requires a level of mental sophistication usually beyond what's available in "space". Teasing will often hurt a submissive in "space" because it can seem like the dominant is displeased when, in fact, he's probably having a great ol' time and is only making a joke. The dominant—who is not in "space"—might even not be aware of this because he sees what is said very differently to the elemental submissive mind. It's usually best to avoid humour or joking when you're dealing with someone in "space". The deeper they are, the simpler things have to be for them.

They don't understand double-bind situations

Again, when not in "space" a submissive might be able to recognise a double-bind situation for what it is, know that it's a game, know that they have been "set up" for failure and just accept it. A submissive in "space" might not get that far in their realisations. The risk here, of course, is that the submissive can get serious feelings of inadequacy or failure because they couldn't do everything that was asked of them, even though it was never expected.

They can't process complex situations

In general, in complex situations, and particularly complex moral or philosophical situations, a submissive in "space" is unlikely to be able to cope or make adequate judgments. They will do the best they can, but the deeper the "space", the poorer the result will be. It is best not to place them in such situations. The advice on many prescription medicines is appropriate here: do not operate heavy machinery or drive automobiles while under this influence.

They can't process complex commands or language

While their adult mind might be quite capable of working out and interpreting any commands you give them, the "in space" submissive mind is more likely to literally interpret commands, and the deeper the "space", the simpler these directives need to be. In other words, they are more likely to do what you say rather than what you mean, so you have to be very careful to say exactly what you mean in words and sentences which they can understand in this simple state of mind. Leave out big words and complicated ethical, moral or philosophical references.

Talk to the submissive, not the adult

Remember that the "in space" submissive and the adult submissive occupy the same body and mind. When talking to the "in space" submissive, use ideas and language to which the submissive can and will respond.

Creating or encountering a situation which is not resolvable by the mental resources and abilities of the "in space" submissive can cause the "adult" mind to wake up to deal with it. This then displaces the sub-space (i.e. pushes it aside). That is, it can cause a rude awakening from sub-space. This is generally not desirable.

Conclusion

You can't communicate with a submissive the same way all the time. While in any general person-to-person conversation, you would have to take into consideration the current mood and circumstances of the person you're talking to, when you're talking with a submissive you also have to take into account their headspace and their reaction to you as a dominant. So, it's not enough to just say what you mean. You have to say what they will interpret—in whatever state of mind they are in—the way you mean. The lot of a dominant is not easy.

My own approach is to recognise that I have—in a way—at least two people to deal with. One's the adult submissive, and the other is the submissive reacting to me, the dominant. This second submissive is the one in a different sort of headspace than the adult, and is the one who has to be treated accordingly. Indeed, failing to recognise the different needs of a submissive in "space" is, I think, one of the big ways you can mishandle them.

Things to think about

1. Look back over your experience with submissives. What expressions, such as "Good girl!" or "Good boy!", have you used when they were in sub-space, which you know would have a bad effect (e.g. pissing them off mightily) when they're not in sub-space?

2. What communication problems have you had with a submissive in sub-space? Have there been times when your submissive misunderstood something which they would have easily understood when not in sub-space? How did you recover the situation?

3. What skills does your current submissive lose when in sub-space? Ability to focus? Ability to verbalise? Physical coordination?

3.3 Person-to-person

A large proportion of the communication between any two people, dominants and submissive included, is both non-verbal and non-conscious. Words and gestures would seem to be conscious forms of communication and, generally speaking, they are. But always, at the same time as we're making a conscious effort to express ourselves, our subconscious and unconscious minds are doing just the same. For a time, not long ago, there was a rash of books on body language. What is body language other than how we communicate when we think we're not communicating?

Here is a short list of some ways in which our subconscious and unconscious minds can participate in our conversations:

1. By affecting our breathing,

2. By influencing our choice of words and phrases,

3. By influencing our tone of voice, the volume of our voice, and our speech rhythm,

4. By modifying our posture or physical attitude towards the person with whom we are speaking (e.g. crossing our arms, or leaning towards or away from the person),

5. By modifying or controlling the gestures we make,

6. By controlling our facial expressions.

Now, all these things are perceivable by the person we're talking to. They aren't necessarily going to be focussing on all of them consciously, so it's mostly left up to their subconscious and unconscious minds to interpret and act on what they receive from us.

When a dominant is expressing themselves to their submissive, there are more ways than the above list suggests in which the dominant's own subconscious or unconscious can get messages across without the dominant necessarily being aware of it. Here are a few:

1. The choice of implement, number and rate of strokes and the dominant's physical attitude when striking or punishing the submissive,

2. How attentive the dominant is to the submissive,

3. The amount of eye contact and physical proximity when talking to them,

4. How tolerant or flexible the dominant is when correcting the submissive,

5. The tone of voice used when giving instructions,

6. How detailed the instructions are. That is, how much freedom the dominant gives the submissive to carry out the instructions,

7. How busy the dominant keeps the submissive.

I like to think that being a master is about mastering yourself first. A part of this is recognising how both your subconscious and unconscious minds work. As your subconscious and unconscious aren't generally directly accessible, observing yourself when you are interacting with others, and taking note of what you do, and taking note of your own reactions, are good ways of collecting information about these normally hidden parts of yourself. Knowing about your subconscious and unconscious—knowing their reactions, quirks, foibles, tics and peccadillos—lets you take control of what they communicate.

Ultimately, your goal is to not just to control what you consciously say to your submissive, but to also take control of what your subconscious and unconscious say to them. Although you can't just reach in to either of them and twiddle them so they do what you consciously want, you can—as I've said earlier in this book—modify or compensate for their effects on you. This includes their effect on your communication.

For example, suppose that when you are feeling testy, stressed or irritated, that you subconsciously tend to stand closer to and over your submissive. Knowing this and recognising these feelings within you, would let you consciously decide to stand further back if what you're consciously trying to communicate to your submissive is not meant to be as intense as it would otherwise appear.

Level-to-level

I don't want it to seem like I'm suggesting here that you should be constantly trying to rein in what your subconscious and unconscious are trying to say. Instead I want you to be able to take control of them and use them to your advantage.

Because, generally speaking, we've all grown up in the same society with the same standards of behaviour, our subconscious minds have all learned and developed along the same lines. They all tend towards the same way of expressing the same emotions and feelings, such as expressing anger by shaking your fist, or by making a gesture at the object of your anger, or by scratching your head if you're confused. Our subconscious minds have also all learned to recognise these same things coming from others.

At the same time, the unconscious of each of us has evolved to recognise and respond to certain behaviours in others (e.g. reactions to pain, fear, anger, affection, and so on.)

Because of this, your submissive's subconscious and unconscious are tuned to a large extent to your own just by virtue of being human and by having grown up in the same society. By taking control of what your own subconscious and unconscious say—by limiting or amplifying them—you can also take more control of your submissive's subconscious and unconscious reactions to you.

Conclusion

Your subconscious and your unconscious <u>always</u> enter into any conversation or communication you have with anyone. Learning the nature of these other parts of you, and learning how to use them, gives you both more control over yourself, and more possibilities for taking control of your submissive.

Communication is about effecting change in the person you are communicating with. Extending your communication armoury to include not just conscious words and gestures, but to also include techniques for reaching into the subconscious and unconscious of your submissive, means that there is one more area of them into which you can reach and take hold… and isn't this what it's all about?

Things to think about

1. Try to pay attention to the differences in how you behave towards your submissive when you've, say, had a stressful day at the office compared to, say, how you behave towards them on the weekend,

2. If you give them an instruction or a task and they do it differently to how you expected, even though you're sure

you actually said the right thing to them, reflect on how you were <u>feeling</u> and how you gave your instructions at the time,

3. When you want to add some intensity or passion into what you are saying to your submissive, to really drive the point or the directive home, don't just raise your voice. Reach into yourself, look at and feel what your subconscious or unconscious minds are feeling, look at their intensities as you speak and let them out,

4. What other ways are there to either restrain or unleash your subconscious or unconscious onto your submissive? What can you do to stir them up? Do certain movies do it for you? Types of food? Or can you do it to order by creating situations in which your subconscious or unconscious will react the way you want?

3.4 Three

> *An Englishman, an Irishman and a Scotsman go into a pub. They go up to the bar and each orders a Guiness. The drinks arrive, each with a thick foamy head on top of the dark brew. The drinkers reach out to take their glasses, but just as they do, three flies—which have been circling above the bar—drop, one into each glass. The Englishman eyes the hole in the foam on his Guiness and pushes the glass away in disgust. The Irishman instead reaches into his glass, grasps the fly between thumb and forefinger, throws it aside and then starts to drink his Guiness. The Scotsman too reaches into his glass and pulls out the fly, but instead of throwing it aside, he shakes it vigorously above his glass yelling, "Spit it out! Spit it out!"*

Have you ever noticed how often things work in threes? We say things like, "When I count to three, we go." Why not two? Why not four? When trying to date a girl, guys will generally accept up to three, "I have to wash my hair," or, "My grandparents are coming over"-type excuses before giving up. There are three lamps in a traffic signal. There are examples of three everywhere.

What's important is that three of anything is often enough to reliably recognise the beginning of a pattern.

Humour tends to work via unexpected twists and the above joke uses the Englishman and the Irishman to establish the beginning of a pattern and a sense of expectation. At the same time, we're made to wonder what's going to happen when the Scotsman is brought into play. Here's the same joke with the Englishman and the Irishman removed. Is it as funny?

> *A Scotsman goes into a pub. He goes up to the bar and orders a Guiness. The drink arrives, with a thick foamy head on top of the dark brew. He reaches out to take the glasses, but just as he does, a fly, which has been circling above the bar, drops into his glass. The Scotsman reaches into his glass, pulls out the fly and shakes it vigorously above his glass yelling, "Spit it out! Spit it out!"*

When we rationalise a series of events, we look at one or two occurrences and say that, OK, the first time could have just been an accident and the second time might have been a coincidence. From the third time on, it's now likely that we're seeing a pattern. Indeed, statistically-speaking we're probably right.

Mother Nature is a good implementer of strategies to cope with the environment. The normal conditioning[1] which occurs in us, and in other animals, to adapt us to the environment, tends to kick in at about the third time something happens to us. In the same way that we become suspicious when something happens twice, and then become mostly certain the third time, Mother Nature's creatures (including us) also start unconsciously to react strongly from about the third time something happens.

What does this have to do with control?

Well, when you are looking to condition a submissive, or to draw out a strong or deep reaction to something, then three is your friend. For example:

---

[1] Including Classical or Pavlovian conditioning as well as adaptation. Pavlov's dog experiment was to ring a bell each time he gave the dogs food. After a few trials the dogs would salivate automatically when they heard the bell, even if they were given no food at the time.

1. If you want to physically take control of a submissive you can just say, "Stand up!", but it'll be stronger if you give three orders, like, "Stand up! Lift your head up straight! Shoulders back!"

    If you just say, "Stand up!" then there might be some doubt about what you intend to do with the submissive. It might be that you just want a better look at them, after which you'll let them go back to whatever it was they were doing. Giving three orders makes it clear—you are taking control,

2. If you want to take control in a more primal manner—so that they feel it more than just consciously—then you'd take them by the hair or neck and push them to their knees, pull their head up straight, and use your foot to move their knees apart. This is, again, three separate actions,

3. If you're using a cane or some other striking implement on the submissive the first stroke is going to impact them consciously, and the third and subsequent strokes are going to impact them primally. In other words, while they can consciously process a single stroke of the cane as punishment for some evil deed, after three or more strokes their unconscious will kick in whether they like it or not,

4. If you want a submissive to perform some particular task as part of their service, then having them do the task three closely-spaced times will make it clear that this task isn't just some whim—it's something that they need to pay attention to for the long term,

5. When you are conditioning a submissive to respond automatically in some way—like to orgasm when they hear the opening bars of Beethoven's Fifth Symphony—then it will only be from about the third time that you associate the

music with the orgasm that they'll "see" the relationship between the two and start learning subconsciously.

There are, as I've mentioned, other factors beyond just having the three *whatevers*—orders, actions or events—happen. There must be a temporal—or time—relationship which the submissive can see (consciously, subconsciously or unconsciously). If one of these *whatevers* happened last week, another on Tuesday and then the last one today, the submissive might not see the connection.

One consequence of this is that the three things might need to occur close together to be recognised as belonging together.

On the other hand, the three *whatevers* could instead have a temporal relationship with some other significant event that occurs from time to time. These other events could be anything. They could be visits by the dominant, orders, sexual intercourse, outings, meals, anything. For example, if the each time the dominant visits the submissive, he orders her to her knees as soon as he comes in the door, then from about the third visit she'll start to respond automatically, even if this response is just a subconscious preparation for the order, and even before the order is given.

The context in which the *whatever* occurs needs to be the same for the submissive to recognise a pattern and respond to the conditioning. In other words, what's happening around the submissive should not confuse them about the pattern. The same actions done in different physical locations, for example, may make it unclear that there is a pattern intended. This may or may not affect the primal effect of the sequence—because physical location is often less important than sensation to the unconscious—but it could easily confuse the submissive consciously.

It's important to note that context is different at the conscious and at the primal/unconscious levels. At the conscious level, the context is going to include what the submissive is thinking, how they feel about the people near them, worries, what people are saying, what they think they're expected to do, and so on. At the primal level the context is a lot more simple and includes temperature, their level of sexual arousal, any anger or fear they might be feeling, use of physical force, etc.

Conclusion

I think that the most important thing you can take away from this section—forgetting about the number three for the moment—is the realisation that what you do with your submissive can reach different parts of their minds depending on how you do it. For me, one of the great satisfactions is reaching deep into someone, looking at the different levels of their mind, working out what makes it tick, and then making it tick the way I want.

Things to think about

1. Reflect on things you do with your submissive which you do in threes.

2. Think about other things you do with your submissive? Are any of them intended to cause a primal, or animal, response in them? Do you do this consciously?

Chapter 4

Management

In short-term control-taking exercises—let's say those of a day or less—the issues are simply about taking and giving control. There is no need for more. Control is taken, used and then given back.

In longer-term control-based relationships, many other issues start to become important. Certainly control is still there, but long-term management of the submissive also needs to be considered.

In this chapter I want to look at some of the processes involved in keeping control on the rails over a long period of time—such as performance and satisfaction reviews (of both the submissive <u>and</u> the dominant), structures to allow the dominant 24-hours/7-days-per-week control, and issues which appear only in the long-term, such as hunger/need management and ownership.

I refer to *relationships* throughout this chapter's sections. It might be easy to think that I am referring to romantic relationships in some instances, but this isn't the case. A control-based relationship can have everything to do with control, and with dominance & submission, but nothing to do with love. The important thing to remember is that we are dealing with needs and hungers for control. Love might be desirable, but before desires can enter into the equation, the needs and hungers must first be satisfied. It is entirely possible that a dominant and submissive have only mutual respect for each other, but still find the relationship satisfying from a control perspective without love and without friendship.

So, in the rest of this chapter, take *relationship* to mean the dominant & submissive, or control-sensitive, aspects of the relationship between the two individuals. Whatever else there may be between them, is a topic for some other book.

4.1 Two different types of control

The control and attitude you have when you meet and have a scene with a submissive at a casual play party, compared to the control and attitude you need to have in a long-term relationship with a submissive, are very different. For a start, at a party:

1. You will be full-on (i.e. actively) dominant towards your submissive for the whole time,

2. The control you have is extremely limited and, correspondingly, the responsibility you bear is also extremely limited,

3. You can, and possibly will, be walking away at the end of the scene and never see this particular submissive again,

4. If things don't seem to be working out, you can always end the scene early,

5. It's very exciting, but not necessarily <u>deeply</u> satisfying.

On the other hand, in a long-term relationship with a submissive:

1. You aren't full-on dominant all the time. Sometimes, possibly for long periods, you are an ordinary mortal. Instead of being focussed 100% of the time on holding your submissive in your sway by your intense gaze and your firm and authoritative voice, sometimes you are just chatting to friends, having a nap on the couch, taking a shower or watching TV,

2. The control you have and assert over your submissive is much more extensive—including influence over your submissive's career choices, finances, health care, friendships, family involvements and children—with correspondingly extended responsibility,

3. You won't be walking away at the end of the scene, because for you and your submissive, the scene never really ends. Even when you aren't with your submissive, the awarenesses and the control doesn't stop,

4. If something isn't working, or if you get bored or lose interest, or if you get really annoyed or angry, you don't have the freedom to walk away. You must stay and deal with it,

5. Short scenes can still be very exciting, and the use of your control, and seeing the growth of your submissive and your relationship, can be deeply satisfying.

While you might be able to take and wield control in a scene, your control-sensitive submissive is also going to want and need to feel your control over the relationship itself in the long term. In other words, your skill and ability in directing your submissive how to kneel, how to walk, how to serve you food and drinks, and how to perform your favourite sexual gymnastics is one thing; but your ability to take hold of the relationship, to deal with differences between you and your submissive, to set a direction for you both and keep the relationship on that particular track, is what will give both you and your submissive that feeling of having a much deeper and more solid control base.

Another thing to consider is that the act of control-taking is typically very brief. Creating a scene specifically to take control from your submissive is mostly going to be short and intense. Actually asserting that control is something done almost at leisure once you have control. In a long-term relationship, you could probably expect that most of the time you'll be using control you already have, rather than spending any great amount of time actually taking control.

Another way of looking at the difference between short, party-scene activities between a dominant and a submissive, and the activities of the same individuals in a long-term relationship, is that the proportion of control-taking and control-giving compared to control-using is higher in short-scenes than it is in long-term relationships.

Conclusion

The control experienced during short scenes is usually intense and has a clear start and end. In contrast, the control that exists in a long-term relationship can be more subtle or low-key, and has no start or end. Both types of control are important parts of the dominant & submissive mix.

Things to think about

1. In a long-term relationship, the dominant and submissive are likely to do control-based scenes from time to time. How do these short, and often intense, control-based scenes fit into the larger picture of their long-term control-based relationship? Does the dominant take more control during these short scenes and give it back at the end of the scenes, or is it simply that the dominant asserts control they already have. Or is it something else?

2. Given that control-sensitive submissives need to feel controlled, how effective is long-term control at providing this feeling? Or is long-term control more a comfort which needs to be periodically reinforced with short and intense scenes of control assertion?

4.2 Planning and management

Being in control of your submissive when you are actually physically present is straight-forward. Directing how they serve, what they wear, or any of the activities in which they might be involved in at the time, is just a matter of issuing the appropriate orders. In this sort of *immediate* environment, both you and your submissive get an immediate reward: they feel directly controlled and you feel directly in control.

To extend this feeling of control into the long-term requires that you take control of the long-term. This means knowing what you want, planning how to get there and then managing yourself, your submissive and the relationship so that you get on course and stay on course to that goal.

In this section, I want to look at planning and management of a long-term relationship with a submissive, focussing on some of the things that you need to be particularly aware of along the way.

4.2.1 Planning

One of the first things that I want to point out is that this is, of course, all about control; more precisely it's all about control, and the awareness and the feeling of control. This awareness and the feeling of control are largely what distinguishes your relationship with your submissive from any other sort of relationship with someone. This awareness of control and your strategies for exploring, taking, and asserting control should be fairly high up in your list of things-to-consider once you start planning.

Planning has two important parts:

1. Working out what you want and,
2. Working out how to get it.

This first part, working out what you want, can come even before you've met this new and exquisite creature who is to become your submissive. In this stage of planning you should first be considering what you want out of the relationship:

1. Is it an opportunity for you to get experience or to learn?
2. Is it for sex?
3. Do you want someone for service? If so, what kind of service? Personal assistant, house-cleaner, gardener, whore, supplier of sexual orifices?
4. Are you looking for an outlet for your dominant drive or for your need to control?
5. Do you enjoy training, and are you looking for someone to train or mould?
6. Are you looking for an emotional involvement?
7. Are you looking for someone who is strong and opinionated, or someone pliable and quiet?
8. Are you looking for someone into bondage or pain?
9. Are you looking for someone challenging?
10. Are you looking for playfulness?
11. Are you looking for someone as an outlet for your sadism or cruelty?

12. Are you looking to start a family with your submissive?

The above list falls into the category of what you want to get. On the other hand you also need to consider what you want to give. Submissives have their own wants and needs, of course. These can range from purely vanilla-type needs—such as affection, sex, company, attention, etc.—to submissive needs—such as the need for control, pain, sex, etc. If you have a submissive who needs to feel fairly extensive control, and you are looking only to give light or occasional control, or a form of control which doesn't satisfy them, then there will be friction and dissatisfaction on both sides. The sorts of things that I listed in the "get" list above can give you a clue, but here are some other things which your submissive might be wanting or needing you to give:

1. A demanding relationship in which they can feel themselves pushed,

2. The opportunity to learn more about themselves,

3. The opportunity to serve,

4. An intellectual challenge,

5. Bondage.

Management

Management is a process. It's what you do to get you to your goal. It's also what you use to take and keep control in the long term. The first step is the one I've already talked about under Planning. You need to work out what your goal is, and who you want to take there with you.

Interview

Having a formal interview or two can set the tone for a formal relationship based on more than the occasional scene. Ostensibly, the interview, or interviews, is used for you both to communicate wants and needs, for you to learn about this submissive, find out what about them works for you, and what you might have problems with. But at the same time, you will be answering their sometimes-unvoiced questions about where you will be taking them. Importantly, you will be (or should be) taking control of the future of the relationship, should it come to pass.

Openness and generosity of information are important during the interviews. The more each of you reveals at this time, the fewer surprises there will be later, and the more you will each be able to trust each other. This relationship is going to be a joint effort with both of you working towards common goals. Any confusion or wrong ideas will carry forward into the expectations which are inevitably and necessarily created, and can possibly cause one or both of you to be dissatisfied later.

That's not to say, of course, that one or both of you won't feel dissatisfied in the relationship later anyway. As the relationship develops, you should expect that you'll learn things about yourself and your wants which might cause you and your submissive to grow apart rather than to grow together. This too, is something you need to be open about.

You might not have a sit-down or formal interview, and instead effectively do the same thing over a number of more casual meetings. Regardless of how you do your interviews, here are some things that you might want to know from a potential submissive:

What are their long-term goals? How well their goals fit in with their service to you and your own goals will help determine how long your relationship might last. Are they looking to improve their current service skills or acquire new ones? Are they looking to better understand themselves? Are they looking for some other win now or in the future as a result of their time with you? Do they view this as an apprenticeship on their way to becoming a dominant themselves?

What about their limitations? Do they get jealous? Do they have ongoing medical problems or physical limitations like allergies, diabetes, injuries, permanent disabilities, etc.? Do they have any overriding family commitments like a sick parent, brother or sister, or do they need to provide support of some kind to a single-parent sibling? What about their education? Does it match up with yours? Do they have any psychological problems, like a history of sexual abuse as a child, or have they had bad experiences with previous dominants, which might impact their service? What about any problems, such as coordination difficulties, related to physical skills? Do they have problems with handiwork, for example, or with cooking?

As a submissive, what rewards are effective for them? Do they respond well to compliments? Attention? Physical or verbal stroking or petting? Is giving them free time a reward? Is good food or good sex a useful reward?

Beyond finding out which rewards work for them, also find out the negative, or down-side, of each reward? Can they get too much of a reward? Can they become spoiled?

What can you use to punish them? Pain? What sort of pain? Is it enough to simply show them that they have disappointed you? Confinement? Isolation? Bread and water? Removing control, i.e. making them decide for themself or taking structure away from them?

Just as you need to learn the down side of rewards, you also need to learn the down side of punishments. Can this submissive become bitter? How do they need to be treated after punishment to get them back on the rails again?

Ask them the best ways of training them. What sort of things can they be trained to do? What sort of things can't they be trained to do? Does trying to teach them dog tricks (such as sitting up or begging) strike at their self-image too deeply, and is the end result bad feeling, resentment or humiliation? Does punishment-and-reward work? What about repetition? How well can they stay focussed? What can motivate them to learn better? Will smiles from you work?

What skills do they already have that can be useful to you? Can they cook? Can they balance your accounts? Can they repair or tune your car? Can they build furniture? Can they advise you on investments? Do they have medical training? Can they write? Can they sing, dance or play an instrument?

Find out about their previous experience as a submissive. Find out what variety of services or training they've had in the past, and how different their previous dominants were from each other. This will give you an idea of how quickly they can learn and how flexible they are. While you're at it, of course, find out why they parted company with their previous dominants.

Learn what they need. This is distinct from what they want. They might need pain regularly, or a strong hand keeping them tightly under control. Maybe they also need some emotional connection with their dominant, regular opportunities to orgasm, time on their own, regular physical activity and so on. When you know what their needs are and why they're interested in you as someone who can satisfy them, then you also need to work out how you, as distinct from any other dominant, can satisfy them to suit you both best.

What are the consequences of their needs not being met? Do they act out? Do they lose focus and become sloppy? Do they become irritable or emotional? Do they have trouble sleeping or responding sexually? Learn the symptoms so that you can recognise them.

Another thing to consider in the needs department, is can their needs be used or manipulated (like letting them build up) to motivate them in training, or to assert control over them?

Finally, in any such interview process there needs to be some

negotiation. Is this going to be a fixed-length contract? Are there any limitations to which you both agree—such as time off for family, some financial considerations, or goals for the submissive to achieve—as part of the basis for entering into the relationship?
It might be a good idea to keep notes.

Evaluation

After the interviews, you need to consider how well this submissive is going to fit into your plans. At the same time, this submissive is going to be working out how well you will fit into their plans. They might be expecting to be controlled—maybe as completely as possible. Regardless of how much control you eventually take, they will still have needs which must be satisfied, and they will still also have an idea of the direction that they want to take.

Whether you decide to take on this submissive or not, should depend on how well you think they will satisfy your needs and wants and how well you think their needs and wants will be satisfied.

I suppose you could be lucky, or persistent, enough to find a submissive who appears to be a perfect fit for your goals. If not though, you might need to review, modify or even scrap your initial plans and come up with something new. And, just because you spent a lot of time working these plans out, doesn't mean that you shouldn't create new ones should a submissive come along whose characteristics promise equal or better reward by following a different path.

Acceptance and induction

If all goes well during the interview and the evaluation steps, then congratulations! You have yourself a new submissive. At this point you have some hard work to do. This is mainly going to be taking control of those aspects of your submissive necessary to get them, you and the relationship itself heading in the direction you want.

Initially, there will probably be a period of confusion and possible resistance (conscious or subconscious) as old directions are changed and new ones adopted by both of you. Learning to interact with your submissive, learning their quirks, learning how they interpret what you say and do, are all part of this phase. They will also be learning about you at the same time.

When you get a new job there is an induction. In the same way, in this early phase of your relationship, there is also an induction [hopefully] designed to get your submissive and, to a lesser extent you, off on the right foot.

A submissive needs this. It is a chance for you to take and assert control by laying down basic expectations and behaviours. Here are some examples of what you might want to cover with them:

1. Introduction to where they're going to be working or performing, and what training they are going to receive,

2. Introduction to duties—including how to behave towards you and towards visitors, how to do regular tasks, etc.,

3. Introduction to other colleagues, and to any other submissives they are likely to spend time with,

4. Setting up their initial timetable,

5. Explanation of your timetable,

6. Explanation of the use of basic equipment, like the coffee machine, washing machine, refrigerator, telephone or fax, vibrators, etc.

Both during the induction phase, and later on in the relationship, you need to provide your submissive with training time. This will most likely be time which they'll think of differently to the time when they're actually working or performing. It's important that you impress on your submissive that training is just as much of a duty as their other work. You also need to provide *quality time*, when you're free of distractions, to supervise and work with them during training sessions. Just as much as your submissive needs to see that you value their productive service, your investment of your own time and energy into their training, shows how important that it is to you as well.

Make sure that they understand, if appropriate, the goals of their training. It's usually much more effective if your submissive knows what to work towards, and on what to focus, rather than just having what they see as aimless exercises to perform.

Ongoing

Once the new direction is set and everyone involved is accustomed to the new "ways", you'll start doing the good bits which you anticipated in your planning. You'll be training your submissive, using them and getting to know them better, within the framework of this now-stable relationship.

Things aren't going to always go smoothly, and there will be unfortunate or unanticipated crises to deal with, and unexpected limits in either yourself or your submissive to which to adapt, and so on.

Mostly, if you've done your planning fairly well, and have interviewed in depth, there will be few surprises, and those that appear should be relatively easy to deal with.

On a relatively frequent basis you could be expecting to do things like:

1. Monitor your submissive's progress,

2. Provide them with feedback on the quality and acceptability of their work or performance,

3. Provide one-on-one supervision to help satisfy their need to feel controlled, and to satisfy your need to feel in control,

4. Help them with tasks or with their training when they're having trouble,

5. Discipline or punish them.

Review and redo

At intervals, and possibly also during difficult times, you'll need to step back and look at the progress you, your submissive and the relationship are making. Open discussions with your submissive at these times are important so that you can make sure that they feel they are getting their needs met, and that they are happy with the progress. Even if things are running smoothly, an order here or a duty there might be able to be tweaked so that things run even better.

If things aren't running smoothly, then something more than tweaking will be required. Try and identify what isn't working. Setting a different direction, or even finding a new goal and re-planning everything, aren't out of the question. There are many cycles within long-term relationships—this is one of them: the regular review and refinement of progress.

It's probably not going to be completely obvious on day one how well your relationship with your submissive is going to work out, or how well they are going to perform for you with the tasks, duties and structure you give them. In the longer term, you need to devote some time, maybe monthly or weekly, to reflecting on the progress they are making and make any necessary changes. Things to consider are: your submissive's attitude, the quality of work they do, their general performance, conflicts with others, how well your own goals are being met, and how well your submissive's goals are being met.

It's often worthwhile to talk to them even if you don't perceive any problems, because maybe they do. When you do have talks like this with them, do your best to make sure they can say what's on their mind, rather than having them bound by any communication rules, or by feelings, to say only what's acceptable.

As an outside observer, you may be able to see characteristics or behaviours in your submissive which they either don't see, or which they maybe see as more or less significant than they really are. Part of what you do over the longer term, is look at what you discovered from your submissive during the interview phase, and then compare it to what you actually see and experience with them. Even if there seems to be a serious difference between the two, it doesn't mean that they were lying to you or trying to manipulate you during the interview. Their own perception of themselves is certainly going to be different to what you perceive, and the impact which you, as a person and dominant, the structure you impose, and the tasks and duties your submissive performs for you, are all going to bring out different characteristics in them.

Counselling

There are going to be problems. If your submissive is not performing to your expectations, or they're not happy, then you, as the dominant-in-control, are in the hot seat, and it's your job to get the problems resolved. It might be a problem with your submissive, it might be a problem with you, it might be a problem with both of you, or it could just be a mismatch which can never be resolved.

What you need to do is talk. Reflect. Discuss it with your submissive. Listen to what they say. Just because they know the answer to a problem and you don't, doesn't mean that they're in control or that you lose face. Remember that your submissive is a resource for you to use, even one to use to solve problems between you.

If necessary, get someone else involved who has more experience. After all, the best sort of dominant is one who will get the problems solved, rather than one who tries to do it all themselves and messes it up.

Especially recognise that you might have to be the one who changes, and that it might have been a bad expectation on your part which lead to whatever problem you are [both] experiencing.

Termination

For any number of reasons you might decide to release your submissive. Maybe you're both growing in different directions, maybe your agreed time together is up, or maybe there was just a mismatch. Here are some things to think about:

1. Do it smoothly so that there is minimum bad feeling and minimum damage to the submissive's ego. Don't say, "You're not useful to me any more. Go away." If they don't already know, explain why it's happening,

2. Remember that some emotional bonding may have occurred, and that you simply need to be gentle as a person with them,

3. After anything more than a couple of days under your control, your submissive will need some time to get used to being in control again. Don't just kick them out the door, but instead give them back control slowly—maybe over a period of couple of days or even weeks—and let them get used to making decisions and choosing their own direction again. Be available for advice for some time after they leave, especially if you have been dealing with things like insurance or bills which they now need to take over,

4. Teach your submissive, or explain to them what you've learned about them, so that they know themselves better,

and so that they can carry that information to their next dominant. Maybe even document it for them. Be available as a reference.

Conclusion

I can't stress how important it is for you, as a dominant, to assert your control through the management of your relationship with your submissive. Just directing isolated activities—such as kneeling, serving, how they dress, etc.—is not all which you can do. You taking control of the relationship is a way for your submissive to feel that they themselves are cupped in your hands, to feel your control enclosing them, and is also how you can feel your control permeating your own life.

In this section I have mentioned a number of situations in which you can take and assert control over the relationship, but in truth there are opportunities at all times from the beginning to the very end.

Things to think about

1. Taking control is equal to taking responsibility. When you have a relationship with a submissive, how much control do you need to take? How much, instead, do you want to take?

2. How often and in what form does the control need to be?

3. How flexible can you be in regards to how much, what form and how often?

4. What does your list of priorities for a relationship with a submissive look like? Where does control come on the list?

5. Can you list times and occasions other than those I've mentioned in this section, where you have the opportunity to assert control over your submissive or the relationship?

6. What happens to the nature of a relationship which progresses from occasional scenes at parties, to living together?

4.3 Ritual

> *OED. Ritual. n. A prescribed order of performing religious or other devotional service.*

Rituals are about symbols. Some rituals are completely symbolic—such as when a submissive bows their head as their dominant enters the room, or when they kneel at the feet of their dominant—or they can add flavour to useful duties and tasks—such as how a submissive addresses their dominant, or how they serve food or drinks to their dominant.

While tasks and duties have, almost by definition, a certain amount of usefulness involved, rituals—or the ritualistic components of tasks and duties—are not particularly useful at all... at least, not in a physical sense. Kneeling and grovelling, while possibly psychologically rewarding for both the submissive who performs it, and for the dominant at whose feet the submissive grovels, is not of any physical benefit. On the contrary, the submissive might even get the dominant's shoes dirty or leave lip marks on them which would have to be cleaned off later.

The work involved in cleaning a dominant's house is also not inherently ritualistic, but can have ritualistic components, e.g. kneeling at the foot of the dominant's bed for a moment before changing the sheets. And some work can be hard to ritualise—mopping the floor might be an example of one such.

Two of the characteristics of a ritual, are that it is performed more than once, and that it has a well-defined (or *prescribed*) way of being done.

Ritual is a vital part of the relationship between a dominant and their submissive. One of the roles which rituals play is that they allow the nature of the submissive's relationship to the dominant to be expressed. Just standing around knowing that they are submissive, is usually not enough to satisfy any need or desire the submissive might have. Being able to feel it and being able to express it both to themselves and to their dominant can, on the other hand, be very satisfying indeed. A ritual can directly satisfy the need for a submissive to express their submissive nature[1].

A submissive will create their own rituals as part of the way they naturally express their feelings towards their dominant or towards their relationship. Exactly what form these self-created rituals will have will vary from submissive to submissive. They will still be—as all rituals are—actions performed the same way each time, and could be things like attitudes or postures adopted in relation to the dominant, devotional or respectful behaviour towards objects belonging to the dominant, or certain ways of performing regular tasks given by the dominant.

Rituals mandated by the dominant are different to rituals created by the submissive themselves. Physically they might look like something the submissive could have created for themselves, but because they are given to the submissive by the dominant they have extra potency:

1. They are a gift from the dominant to the submissive in that they give the submissive an extra way of feeling satisfied or rewarded for their behaviour. Just by giving the submissive a ritual to perform, the dominant has, at the same time, created a new way for the submissive to express themselves,

---

[1] Rituals exist in very many forms. Consider a "good" Catholic, for example. They might go to church every Sunday, but the fact that they go to church doesn't inherently make them into a better human-being. They could be just as moral, or just as kind-hearted and generous if they stayed at home, but the regular ritual of going to church is a way of <u>expressing</u> that they are a good and enthusiastic catholic.

2. Because the rituals come from the dominant, the submissive knows and feels first-hand that performing these rituals will be pleasing to the dominant. As distinct from self-created rituals, rituals from the dominant have an aspect of direct service involved in them.
3. A ritual imposed by the dominant is also a form of control imposed by the dominant.

Feedback

Many rituals have an important *feedback* component. What I mean here is that part of the reward or satisfaction which the submissive gets from a ritual, comes from the dominant's reaction to the ritual. For example, the reward for kneeling at the dominant's feet might include, as well as the inner feeling coming from the submissive's own expression of rank, that of getting the "ownership smile" from the dominant, or stroking of the submissive's hair. The dominant's reaction thus reinforces the awareness of the submissive's station expressed by the kneeling.

There isn't always such direct feedback from the dominant, or indeed any at all. Kneeling at the foot of the dominant's bed before changing the sheets is likely to be purely an internal experience for the submissive. The reward here comes purely from the devotional and expressive nature of the ritual, and nothing else.

Context

Doing the same sequence of actions doesn't mean that it is a ritual each time; there is also the context in which the actions are performed to consider. Bowing the head when serving one particular individual might be a ritual, while for other people it is a simply a sign of measured respect. Certain actions might also be rituals at certain times of day or in certain places, but then at other times are just actions. For example, pouring a drink for their dominant at a particular time of day (e.g. evening) might be a ritual, while at other times it is simply respectful. As another example, some religious rituals include a washing of hands. This doesn't mean that every time someone washes their hands that they are partaking in a religious ritual.

Conclusion

You can't be doing dominant things to your submissive all the time, nor can they be doing submissive things to you all the time. Rituals give both you and your submissive ways to express and even reinforce the relationship between you, by means of symbolic acts or symbolic ways of doing ordinary tasks. Feedback, or reacting to the rituals the submissive performs, can be an important way of *feeding* the submissive's needs.

Lastly, rituals dictated by the dominant are symbols of control.

Things to think about

1. What rituals do dominants have in general? What rituals do you personally, as a dominant, have?

2. What rituals does your submissive have or perform? Which ones came from you? Which ones did your submissive create themselves? In what contexts are they rituals, and in what contexts are they just actions?

3. From a control point of view, what sort of rituals do you think your submissive should be allowed to create for themselves? Is control over this something which you feel is appropriate for you to have or assert? Is creating their own rituals a way for a submissive to express control over themselves? Is this a good thing?

4. A ritual can also become a comfortable rut. Should a submissive experience a ritual as something comfortable? Or should a ritual always be at least a little bit of a burden? Does being comfortable affect how well a ritual works?

4.4 Structure

> *OED. Structure. n. An organised body or combination of mutually connected and dependent parts or elements.*

> *PM[2]. Structure. n. A way for a dominant to provide control over a submissive in the dominant's absence.*

When you are physically present, it is easy for your submissive to feel that they are under your control. If you aren't actually directing them at any particular time, they can defer to you when decisions need to be made, and they can simply ask you what you wish to be done when they're idle. Control is on tap for them when you're around. Naturally enough, this is a very good thing for a control-sensitive submissive.

What happens when you leave the room? Or go to work? Or—if they don't live with you—when you send your submissive home? Do they still feel your control?

Most dominants give their submissives standing orders or rules about what to do when they are not around, e.g. no talking to other dominants, no masturbation without permission, etc. In this section I want to look at this form of control—control in the dominant's absence.

---
[2] Peter Masters

It's not the goal of a control-sensitive submissive to take back control from the dominant, but as I mentioned in the earlier section on losing control (page 65), there are situations in which a submissive has to take back control. One of these is when they have no indication from the dominant about what to do in a situation which arises when the dominant is not there.

At such a time the submissive has to decide... and to be able to decide they first must take back control of the decision-making process. This is, as mentioned in that earlier section of this book, bad. Generally, it is also avoidable.

For a submissive to be able to feel the dominant's control when the dominant is not around, and to know what options to choose, how to behave, and what tasks to perform, the submissive requires a well-integrated set of rules, orders, and awareness of the dominant's values and preferences. These all combine to create a structure which encloses the submissive. Ideally, it will provide them with them with constant awareness of the dominant and the dominant's control.

There are four main elements to this structure. They are:

1. Standing orders,

2. Rules,

3. An understanding of the dominant's moral and ethical values,

4. An awareness of the dominant's preferences in a wide range of areas.

Standing orders

A standing order is an instruction or command with a measure of permanence. In other words, standing orders don't expire. They exist until the dominant decides to withdraw them. Most commonly, standing orders tell a submissive what to do either at a particular time, or when some particular event happens.

A standing order might be something like:

> *Each morning, except Sundays, you are to rise at 6am, wash and dress yourself, eat a light breakfast, perform any chores due, including loading and starting the washing machine, and prepare and serve my breakfast in my bedroom at 7:30am. You will then wait until I give you further instructions for the day.*

A characteristic of any order, including a standing order, is that they tell the submissive something to actually do. The example standing order above tells them what to do in the morning up until when they wake their dominant and serve breakfast.

Here's another example of a standing order:

> *During the course of your duties around the house, note down on the shopping list anything that is in short supply. A couple of days before we will run out of anything bring it to my attention.*

The above example seems to be common sense and you might question why you'd even need to give this order at all. There is an important reason though, and that is by making it an order you are taking away choice (i.e. control) from your submissive. You are imposing a standard, and are making them directly answerable to you about this aspect of their performance rather than leaving it up to them.

Rules

Rules, like standing orders, don't expire until the dominant decides to withdraw them. But rather than tell the submissive to do some particular thing, rules serve to modify something that the submissive is already doing or is going to do.

Here's an example of a rule:

> *When I send you on a shopping or similar errand, I do not want you stop for any form of rest or refreshment unless I give you explicit permission beforehand, or unless the errand takes more than two hours. In either case you will only break for fifteen minutes at most, and have no alcohol or more than a light snack.*

This rule doesn't send the submissive off to do anything, but instead imposes limits on what they can do while performing errands. While what a submissive does as a result of an order (standing or otherwise), like a task or errand, has an obvious start and end, a rule applies all the time. It doesn't start and it doesn't end.

Here's another example of a rule:

> *In my absence, and in the company of other dominants who are aware of your station, and with their permission, I want you to actively serve to the best of your ability in all ways except sexually, and in such a way as to bring respect on yourself and to me. With regard to serving sexually, you will not allow any sexual penetration of yourself, and you will not actively touch anyone sexually. Other dominants may touch you as long as it does not involve penetration. You are not to hesitate to physically uncover yourself for them.*

Moral values, ethical values and decision-making

There are going to be times, when you're not around, when standing orders and rules won't cover a situation. Standing orders and rules effectively give your submissive pre-made decisions. When they don't suit the situation, your submissive will have to make decisions on their own. The decisions they make should be aligned with the ones you would make if you were there. There are three parts to making this happen:

1. Teaching your submissive about your moral and ethical values,

2. Teaching them how you go about making decisions, and

3. A standing order.

By teaching your submissive your moral and ethical values, and by filling in the gaps by explaining the steps you take to arrive at different decisions, you equip your submissive with the information they need to make the same sort of decision you would make. This is not simple because there's a lot for them to learn about how you would act in any number of situations. This learning process is a long one and doesn't just consist of you explaining things to them. It consists, probably mostly, of them observing and learning from what you do.

The final part of this is activating this teaching by giving them a standing order such as the following:

> *I have given you a set of rules and standing orders to guide you when I am not around. I do recognise that there will probably be exceptional situations when these rules and orders won't be enough. From now on, in these situations, I expect you to do your best to decide as I would, and to act as I would have you act if I were there.*
>
> *It's now your duty to learn what you need to know to be able to do this. I expect you to learn by observing me and by asking me about my choices, so that you can make the decisions I want made.*

> *Each time you do need to make a decision in my absence, I also expect you to tell me about it as soon as practical so that I can review it and make any necessary corrections for the future.*

In this way, when you aren't around, your submissive will be making choices and decisions based on your values instead of theirs. They will feel this as your control over them. They will also know that these choices are subject to review by you. They are not free choices with no consequences. That doesn't mean that your submissive should be punished if they do their best, but still make a decision that you consider poor. It may just mean that they have more to learn from you, or that you have more to teach them.

Preferences

Sometimes there are simply better ways, from your point of view, for your submissive to behave, and better things for them to choose than others. Your submissive will learn many of these preferences by observation. Others they'll learn by you telling them. Preferences are not a matter of right or wrong, but instead of good or better.

Preferences might be:

1. Your preferred type of tea,

2. The way you prefer your bed made,

3. The amount of detail you are comfortable managing with regard to your submissive.

To help your submissive learn your preferences, there are couple of things you can do:

1. Explain your preferences,

2. Be consistent so your submissive can see patterns in your behaviour and choices.

Conclusion

Creating a comprehensive structure for your submissive consisting of the above-mentioned four elements, allows them to act autonomously while still staying under your control. A good structure will prevent them from ever encountering a situation where they have to take back control.

Such structures aren't built in a day. As you learn what's needed, and you learn about the situations which your submissive encounters, you'll gradually build up a structure in which your submissive feels confident and comfortable, and one which benefits you at the same time.

Over time, bits will get added and bits removed as you and your submissive grow, and as things around you both change.

Things to think about

1. Defining a structure in which your submissive can makes choices in your absence, means that they might make a wrong choice. How do you make sure that they will confidently do their best without being frozen by fear of negative consequences if their choice turns out to be poor?

2. What standing orders do you typically give a submissive?

3. What behavioural rules do you typically give a submissive?

4. Different interpretations might mean that your submissive actually does something different than what you intended when you're not around. Seeing as you're not actually present a lot of the time to see your structure in operation, how do you make sure that your submissive is doing what you want?

5. There is a blurred distinction between preferences based on ethical or moral values, and preferences based on the mood-of-the-moment. Preferences based on ethical or moral values are likely to be unchanging in the long-term, while mood-of-the-moment preferences can possibly fluctuate from one moment to the next. What preferences do you have which are important to your submissive? Which ones are due to a moral or ethical stance on your part, and which are simply stylistic or matters of taste? What factors cause your preferences to change? Do you have preferences for your submissive that change, say, from morning to afternoon? Or on a weekly basis? Or depending on how your day at work has been?

4.5 Ownership

The idea of ownership is an important one in the world of dominance and submission. For some dominants, the ownership of their submissive is a big part of their relationship. Being able to say, "this submissive is mine," and to be able to actually feel their ownership in some way, is part of the reward or satisfaction they feel. Symbols of ownership, such as collars, are used to reinforce this. Even more so for many submissives, it seems that this feeling and awareness of being owned is a critical part of what they look for and crave.

Ownership is not a planet-wide phenomenon. In very primitive cultures being able to own anything at all is simply not possible. They have no concept of ownership. They do not own their clothes, their food, their hunting implements or tools. The key word in this discussion is "concept". Ownership is actually just an idea, one of the many which lubricate the wheels of our own modern society.

You own a car, right? What's the physical connection between you and the car that shows ownership? A piece of paper? No, I don't think that's enough to represent real ownership. What if someone else comes along and says that the car is theirs? You hold up the piece of paper? You get some friends who have seen you driving it? Maybe you get a court to decree that on the basis of the evidence the car is yours?

What it comes down to is there actually isn't any physical thing that you can point to and say, "This is my ownership of the car". You own the car just on the basis of consensus. As long as everyone agrees that you are the owner of the car, then you are.

This idea of an individual being able to own something is very strong in our own society. The idea is so deeply ingrained in us, that we actually treat things like "our" car as being different in some way from every other car. We also accept that we can do things with this car-that-is-no-different-to-every-other-car which we're not allowed to do to other cars.

Indeed, we can own houses, trees, children, cats, dogs, ideas (via patents), bits of earth, kitchen utensils, symbols and designs (via trademarks) and so on. If someone came along and took away one of these things, then the only way we can get it back (barring stealing it back ourselves) is to rely on a majority of other people (society as represented by the courts, for example) agreeing with us that we own it. If they don't agree, then there's nothing else we can assert or use that will get it back. Hence, ownership is a widely-held convention only.

The key to this is consensus. In our society, there are things we are allowed to own and things we can't. Sometimes there are rules which say what we can do with the things we own, and what we can't do. We might own a block of land, for example, but can't build whatever we want on it regardless of how architecturally sound it may be. We have to get society's approval first, e.g. from the local council, planning authority or zoning board. We might own a tree in our backyard, but our local council, as some do, may require us to get permission before cutting it down. What we can do with our pets is limited on humane grounds, and there are many things we simply aren't allowed to own or possess (such as nuclear weapons).

Ownership of a another person is not recognised in our society-at-large. But to delve into some of the deeper forms of dominance and submission, particularly explorations of control, can take you to where the dominant can and must do whatever they want with the submissive. Ideally we'd hope that they'd take full care of the submissive, and do their best to make sure that the submissive stays healthy, whole and useful, but once you get to this point the dominant has *de facto* ownership of the submissive—in the same way the owner of a car can do whatever they want with their car, the owner of a submissive can do whatever they want with the submissive.

Just as ownership of a car, or a house or any other thing, is recognised by our society-at-large, the ownership of a submissive could be recognised by another society (and, indeed, has been in the past). To some extent this already happens in our BDSM world. Dominants and submissives recognise the special relationship between other dominant and submissive couples. Rules of ownership already exist, though these rules vary between groups, which indicate how a dominant should behave, for example, towards someone else's submissive.

Going further, submissives-as-property also exist within our BDSM world. In a similar way to tops, bottoms, submissives and dominants finding their way into a niche of the BDSM world where they can express themselves, these submissives-as-property also find a niche—a society within a community within a society—where they can express themselves, i.e. by being property.

What happens then, if someone believes themselves to be property, to be owned by another person? Regardless of whether you personally think this is possible, or whether you experience it yourself, try this exercise and imagine that you're on the other side of this great ownership conviction: i.e. you are the property. With the same depth that you can accept and act as if you now own a car, you also accept that you are owned, and that your owner has exactly the same rights over you that a car owner has over their car.

When you own the car, then you own it in all respects, and can use it how you want for your advantage. If you own a factory, then you also own what it produces. When you own a person you own what they produce, including their thoughts.

That doesn't necessarily mean that you directly control everything the person does, or that you can directly control their thoughts.

If you own a car or a factory, then you have the right to go and modify it how you choose. If you own a person then you have the same right, don't you?

Conclusion

I suspect that most people see the concepts of control and ownership as being more or less the same thing or, at least, representing the same thing. For a dominant, claiming ownership is the same as saying that they accept that they can do whatever they want with the submissive concerned.

For a submissive this translates to the realisation that they are subject to whatever their dominant decides for them.

Things to think about

1. If ownership is actually a concept, can it be a need? If it isn't itself a need, then what is it that many submissives hunger for when they feel the need to be owned?

2. Where does the ownership of something come from initially? I mean by this that ownership of something can be passed from one person to another *ad infinitum*, but where does it start from? When does a submissive become property that can be owned?

3. How do you express your ownership over your submissive? What do you actually do so that both you and your submissive feel that ownership?

4.6 Delegation

One of the goals of some types of dominant/submissive relationships is the complete taking of control from the submissive by the dominant. The first image that comes to my mind when I start to think about this, is that of a "hobby dominant" who spends his spare time trying to take the last bit of control away from his submissive, a bit like the once-common hot-rod enthusiast trying to squeeze the last RPM or mile per hour out of his pride and joy.

This actually isn't a bad image because, ideally, for a control-sensitive submissive, the more control is taken away from them, the more complete and satisfied they are going to feel. With such a submissive, the dominant is, also ideally, going to be doing their best to ferret out and take away the last vestiges of control their submissive holds.

The word "micromanagement" comes to mind at this point in the discussion. To take as much control as is possible from the submissive, means taking control of all the things which the submissive initially can control themselves. This includes breathing, walking, choice of clothes, how to chew food, toilet excursions, employment, friendships, when and how to wash, what and when to eat and drink, etc., etc.

I'm sure that the average dominant has enough to worry about in their own life, without having to occupy themselves with all the minutae of the life of their submissive as well. However, to do the job of being in control of the submissive properly, the dominant does need to be in control of all those things I mentioned, plus all the rest which I didn't mention.

Actively being in control of all of this 24 hours a day will quickly lose any semblance of being pleasurable for the dominant. So, once the dominant has taken all this control, what do they do with it? Do they then give it back so as not to have it be an unbearable burden for themselves?

Well, they could do it like that, but then the submissive is left in the same state they were beforehand, except maybe with the confidence that their dominant can take control whenever they want to because they've already demonstrated that they can. However—importantly—the submissive isn't under control any more, and so this need in them isn't being satisfied.

The answer to the so-far unasked question of how to keep a submissive under complete control without having to deal with the tiny details of their life is *delegation*. In other words, it involves giving management of some aspects of the submissive's own life and behaviour back to them. After all, the submissive is under control, and is in service to the dominant, and is therefore available for any duties the dominant may care to assign to them—including that of managing the submissive's own life—at least in the short-term.

So, a good answer to the problem of the dominant keeping maximum control while still maintaining their own independence and freedom, is for the dominant to delegate some of the tasks of submissive-management back to the submissive themselves.

This doesn't involve giving control back to the submissive, because the control still ultimately remains with the dominant. The submissive acts simply as the dominant's agent and remains answerable to the dominant. The dominant can, at any time, exercise "executive" control and override the submissive's choices, or redefine the framework in which the submissive is allowed to act.

The difference between giving control back to the submissive and delegating control back to them is important, particularly for the submissive. They must be aware that they aren't getting control back, and that they are being allowed to act only how and while it suits their dominant. The difference is the same as that between, "I have finished deciding how you should dress. In future, you decide for yourself," and, "In future, you are allowed to choose what you will wear, but you will always dress modestly and ensure that you are always well-presented, and that your appearance reflects well upon me."

The first example gives control over how the submissive dresses back to them completely.

The second releases the dominant from having to make all the choices, but leaves the submissive in no doubt that while they have some freedom, it's only to choose in ways of which the dominant approves. As well, because the dominant hasn't released control, they can easily reassert it (e.g. tell the submissive explicitly what to wear) without having to go through the exercise of taking control again because they didn't ever give it back.

Delegating control back to the submissive doesn't completely liberate the dominant, because as the ultimate control-holder they are also the ultimate responsibility-holder. The submissive will be operating according to parameters which the dominant has set, so it's up to the dominant to also ensure that the submissive is working well. This means keeping an eye on them, occasionally fine-tuning the submissive's behaviour and choices, etc.

The dominant also can't escape their own duty to ensure that the submissive feels controlled. In a very real sense, this means flexing the dominant muscles by directly asserting control over the submissive from time to time. For the submissive, it won't be enough that the dominant simply takes control of them once, puts together a set of standing orders, and then lets the submissive go and does nothing further. The submissive has a dominant precisely because they need to feel control. Making choices themselves, even if within parameters set by the dominant, doesn't and won't give them the strong feeling of being controlled that they need.

From time to time then—and the frequency will vary from submissive to submissive, and according to what's happening in the rest of their life—the submissive will need to feel that personal control. This is a type of reinforcement for them. Simply reasserting control, exercising it directly, may well be enough.

One of the risks of delegation is that the submissive might perceive the act of delegation instead as an act of returning control to the submissive. For example, if the dominant says, "From now on you dress yourself as you normally would unless I say otherwise," the submissive might take it to mean that, "You're in control of what you wear now until I decide to take that control back from you."

A possibly better way of having the submissive choose their clothing, but without giving them back control, is to deliberately give them dress guidelines that slightly differ from what they would normally choose for themselves, or to say to them, "In future when you dress, I want you to choose clothes that I would think appropriate for the occasion." This last example then requires the submissive to constantly reflect on their dominant's preferences when choosing clothes—in effect, removing all free choice of clothes from the submissive completely, while only requiring the dominant's occasional attention when they stray too much from the dominant's preferences.

Conclusion

Delegation is a useful tool in long-term management of a submissive. It's a mechanism you can use to retain overall control of an aspect of your submissive's life or behaviour, while not having to micromanage. It may not be the same as hands-on control by you, but it still does maintain your control, while allowing appropriate decisions and choices to be made without you.

Things to think about

1. I have been using the example of choice of clothing as something which you can easily delegate back to your submissive. What other things can you relatively safely delegate back to them?

2. What isn't appropriate for delegation?

3. How can you monitor that delegation is working correctly? How do you know that the right choices are being made?

4. How can you tell whether delegation is being effective at providing you with liberty, while still providing your submissive with the feeling that they are being controlled?

Chapter 5
Discussion topics

Control is a very broad subject. There are many aspects of it which I haven't dealt with for various reasons. Some are too short, maybe too obvious, or maybe too off-topic to rate their own pages. In this chapter I present some of these as discussion topics. Each one has a short introduction, and then a few questions to get you started. Maybe you could get some like-minded friends together and talk about one or two of the topics over coffee.

5.1 Closure

At the end of any activity, regardless of whether it is a once-off scene at a play party, or whether it takes place in the context of a long-term relationship, there needs to be a *closure*. Closure is the process by which all the loose ends are tidied up so that the activity is seen by both participants to be complete. Nothing is left lingering or needing to be dealt with later.

Closure actually occurs much more frequently than just at the end of scenes or relationships. You can find closure at the end of any event or activity. Here are a couple of examples:

1. After a scene negotiation,

2. After a disagreement,

3. After a period of being away from your submissive.

As a dominant, you are seen as the prime initiator within a dominant/submissive relationship. How can you tell that there has been full closure?

1. What can you do to ensure that your submissive feels that there has been full closure?

2. In what situations should you be looking to make sure that there has been closure?

3. If an attempt at closure has failed, what can you do to resolve the situation? What strategies can you use?

4. How do you know when you, personally, experience full closure?

5. How do you know when your submissive experiences full closure?

5.2 Magic

Let me define *magic* as using spells or incantations to influence someone or something. It is a way in which you attempt to assert control over something you don't fully understand, usually by saying the words or doing the things which on previous occasions appeared to cause the outcome you were looking for.

In a way, magic is quite common these days. Lesser word-processor operators know that by clicking here and dragging there they can get their document title to appear in Bold Gothic. If clicking here and dragging there fails to produce Bold Gothic, then they're lost because they only know the magic formula rather than really knowing what they're doing.

Arthur C. Clarke said, "Any sufficiently advanced technology is indistinguishable from magic." We are daily surrounded by technology generally far beyond our understanding. Take microwave ovens, for example. We know the buttons to push, but if the food fails to heat, we have to call in the services of a minor techno-priest who can cause our magic to start working again.

I think that part of the satisfaction of doing something comes from the understanding of it, but if the desired result is reliably achieved without the understanding, then for most people this is just as good.

So, what magic do you use with your submissive? What gestures, phrases or actions do you use because they work, without you really understanding why?

1. Do you do a warm-up of your submissive's backside before

belting into them? Why do you do this? Does it make it better for the submissive? Why is it better?

2. Do you pull your submissive's hair or wrap your fingers around their neck? Why? Because it works?

3. Do you tease your submissive before sex? Why? Why not jump straight in?

4. What other things do you do because they "just work?"

5.3 Satiation

Satiation is about satisfying a hunger or a need. In psychological terms, you might say it is about restoring equilibrium. The hunger might not be a hunger for food. It could be a hunger for sex, for pain, for control, for attention, for physical contact or stroking, or for any of a myriad of other things.

Taking control of when and how a submissive satisfies their needs is a popular way of manipulating a submissive and helping them to feel your control over them. You might, for example, limit their opportunities to experience sexual satisfaction, or you might impose rules on their eating behaviour, or how often you attend to their need for pain.

Ultimately though, a submissive's needs and hungers must be satisfied, at least to a level where the submissive can continue to function. Leaving them too hungry for food, or too hungry for sex, can distract them so much that they can't focus on their tasks.

1. How can you tell when it's time to address your submissive's hunger?

2. Should you attempt to completely satisfy a submissive's hunger or need? Or should you leave them still a little hungry, possibly to keep them motivated, or possibly to remind them that they aren't the one who controls the satiation of their hunger?

3. In what situations is it a positive experience for the submissive for you to manipulate them through their hunger?

4. In what situations is it negative?

5. What hungers does your submissive have which you control?

6. What hungers do you yourself have which you use your submissive to satisfy?

5.4 Humour

I am curious: what role does humour have in a control-based relationship? Throughout this book I've been trying to get rid of the trimmings and expose the core of such relationships. Clearly though, there are many things which can be used as tools, such as sex and pain. What about humour?

1. Can you use humour to assert control?

2. Can you use bad puns to inflict discomfort on your submissive?

3. Can you use humour to release tension when there's stress between you and your submissive?

5.5 Rhythm

How does rhythm enter into your life? Many people find heavy, thumping music excites them and makes their blood rush. Regular, heavy beats at about the same frequency as your heart-rate can be very powerful or empowering. Faster beats can be agitating.

1. Do you use music when you're "working" with your submissive? What sort of music helps you to feel dominant?

2. Is there music which makes your submissive feel submissive?

3. Do you flog your submissive? What works best: regular, heavy, thudding strokes, or light, irregular strokes? Or do you use different types and rates of stroke at different times or with different submissives? When is one style better than the other?

5.6 Feeling controlled

Taking control is the first step. After this comes asserting the control. Both you, the dominant, and your submissive then need to feel and experience the control that exists between you in some ongoing fashion to get ongoing pleasure out of it.

What is the experience of being controlled? Control can be directing or restricting the action of your submissive. This is what they need to feel, and what you need to do.

1. In what ways can you do this?

2. Is setting limits a way of asserting control? Is this a hollow experience for the submissive if you're not around to reinforce it? Does imposing limits work for some submissives and not for others?

3. Is micromanagement an option? Is directing every single aspect of your submissive's behaviour rewarding in any way? How long can you keep it up?

4. Are there some forms of control that are more satisfying when asserted infrequently, and are there some forms of control that are more satisfying the more frequently they are asserted?

5. Is indicating your personal preferences a way of asserting control?

6. What does it feel like to be controlled?

7. What does it feel like to be in control?

5.7 Consequences of orders

Back in the chapter on communication I wrote about clarity of communication, about getting the message across, and about taking charge of communication. For a dominant, the role of communication is often letting the submissive know the dominant's preferences, and to communicate orders and give tasks.

What are the consequences of orders though?

Maybe we could divide orders, or their effects, into two categories:

1. Orders for the benefit of the submissive: those which reinforce the submissive's rank in the relationship and give them the feeling of being submissive,

2. Orders that benefit the dominant: orders which direct the submissive's service to the dominant.

Instructing your submissive to walk one or two paces behind and to one side of you is not uncommon. You might think of it as the mobile version of kneeling because it clearly places the submissive in a submissive position.

But what else can it mean?

For one thing, it places the submissive out of the dominant's sight, and, "I want you out of my sight," is probably not the message which the dominant wants the submissive to get. Similarly, giving your submissive orders not to speak or to limit their speech could send the message that you don't want to hear what they have to say. In both these cases, instead of getting the welcome feeling of control from their dominant they might get a feeling of rejection.

In both the above examples, the order is probably intended mostly for the benefit of the submissive, rather than to be directly of service to the dominant.

1. Can you list the orders, standing or otherwise, which you give your submissive?

2. For each of these orders, who benefits and how? Which of the benefits are direct and which are indirect (i.e. not coming directly from the outcome of obeying the order).

3. How do you ensure that your submissive gets the benefit which you intend from an order?

4. I divided orders into two categories above, but I left out orders that reinforce the dominant's rank in the relationship. How important are these? Can you give examples of such orders?

5.8 Difference between a slave and a submissive

If I were to say that the key difference between a slave and a submissive is that a slave can feel <u>slave</u> only by being used or by being of service to their dominant, while a submissive can feel <u>submissive</u> at other times, would you agree?

1. Does a slave need pleasure?
2. Does a submissive need pleasure?
3. Is being used important?

5.9 Cookbook dominance

A short-term exercise in taking control can be almost a clinical exercise. Follow the steps, analyse the reactions, apply the correct response, and viola! Indeed, there are many standard formulas which will work most of the time and get a suitably positive response from many submissives.

1. Is this mastery though? Or is it cookbook dominance?

2. Is a good dominant one who knows very many recipes?

3. Or is a good dominant one who, like good chefs, has both an understanding and a feel for cooking, as well as a ready repertoire of recipes? Such a dominant would be able to handle "standard" submissives as well as those not so standard. Or doesn't this matter outside of a professional BDSM establishment?

4. And who cares anyway? If you have a dominant and submissive couple who are happy, and all their needs are being met by each other, does it need to be more than a cookbook?

5.10   Less than open

Being open with your submissive is probably a good thing. When they know what your goals are—whether the goals are for you, for them, or for the relationship—they can help you work towards them.

1. Are there times when your submissive doesn't need to know what's going on? When are these times?

2. Are there times when they definitely shouldn't know? In what circumstances does this happen?

3. Are you asserting control over them by keeping them ignorant on some issue?

4. When you aren't keeping them in ignorance, is it possible for them to know too much?

5. Should a submissive hold information back? What are the consequences of doing so? What are the consequences of not holding anything back from their dominant?

5.11 What place love?

A common theme in some, but not all, of the literature and practices of BDSM is the idea of love being a key element in the surrender of a submissive.

1. Is love necessary for a satisfying control-based relationship to work?

2. If not, what can love add to such a relationship?

3. What can love take away from such a relationship?

4. Is submission deeper when there's love involved?

5. Does love affect the level of commitment?

6. Can experiencing love for their submissive weaken or strengthen a dominant?

5.12 Hard and soft limits

People in the BDSM world sometimes talk about *hard limits* and *soft limits*. Hard limits are those, usually applying to some particular activity, which are set by either the dominant or the submissive, and which must not be overstepped, e.g. no exchange of bodily fluids with a casual play partner.

Soft limits, on the other hand, usually indicate some point after which one must proceed with caution. A soft limit, for example, might apply to a pain threshold when the submissive wants to push themselves to ever greater heights of adrenaline-driven ecstasy over a number of sessions.

1. What effects do soft and hard limits have on who is in control?

2. How can hard and soft limits be adjusted or defined so as to have as little effect on the dominant's control as possible?

3. What impact on responsibility can there be when hard and soft limits conflict or collide with control-taking?

4. What similarities and differences are there between limits and safewords?

5. Do the dominant's hard and soft limits have any impact on their control of the submissive?

About the author

Peter Masters lives in Sydney, Australia. To keep the wolves from the door he beats computer networks into submission at a local university. He has had a keen interest in computers and computer programming since he was 12 years of age, and has been fortunate to be able to make a career out of one of his life-long passions.

At the age of 12 he also began his interest in a sport that would eventually take him to Europe for more than seven years; namely, the sport of fencing. During his time in Europe Peter qualified as a Master of Fencing, and through much hard work he also learned to speak both Italian and German fluently.

Exploring domination and control of members of the fairer sex is another life-long passion. Since the mid/late 90's, Peter has written and published a number of articles on dominance and submission. He participates in local conferences, and runs an occasional workshop. For a number of years he also chaired or co-chaired—sometimes-weekly and sometimes-monthly—D&S discussion meetings based in Sydney.

Another interest from his early teens is hypnosis. He has a diploma in hypnotherapy, and is the author of a truly fabulous and desirable book on the recreational use of hypnosis and sex. Since it was first published in 2001 **Look Into My Eyes** has gained very positive reviews. It includes a couple of chapters on BDSM and hypnosis, and is available from Amazon.com.

Peter is also the author of **This Curious Human Phenomenon** (2008), which is "an exploration of some uncommonly explored aspects of BDSM." It is also available from Amazon.com.

Peter enjoys the parry and thrust of enthusiastic debate, discovering or learning new things, and writing enthusiastically about himself in the third person for the about-the-author pages of his books.

Printed in Great Britain
by Amazon.co.uk, Ltd.,
Marston Gate.